DATELINE AMERICA

CHARLES KURALT
DATELINE AMERICA

PHOTOGRAPHS BY MARK CHESTER

HBJ

HARCOURT BRACE JOVANOVICH

NEW YORK LONDON

Requests for permission to make copies of any part of the work should be mailed to:
Permissions, Harcourt Brace Jovanovich, Inc., 757 Third Avenue, New York, N.Y. 10017

The author would like to thank Holt, Rinehart and Winston, Publishers, for permission to quote from "American Names" from BALLADS AND POEMS by Stephen Vincent Benét. Copyright 1931 by Stephen Vincent Benét. Copyright © 1959 by Rosemary Carr Benét. Reprinted by permission of Holt, Rinehart and Winston, Publishers.

Printed in the United States of America

LIBRARY OF CONGRESS CATALOGING IN PUBLICATION DATA
Kuralt, Charles, 1934–
  Dateline America.
  1. United States—Social life and customs—1971–
2. United States—Description and travel—1960–
3. Kuralt, Charles, 1934–   I. Title.
E169.02.K868   973.9   78-22262
ISBN 0-15-123957-6

B C D E

The book design and photographs on pages 12, 143, 182 and 218 by Al Cetta; photographs on pages 52, 101, 107, 120, 162, and 198 by Isadore Bleckman; Photographs on pages 92 and 151 by Charles Kuralt; photograph on page 137 courtesy of CBS News; photograph on page 158 courtesy of Lake Havasu City Chamber of Commerce; photograph on page 173 courtesy of Tuskegee Institute; photograph on page 194 courtesy of the Grand Hotel, Mackinac Island; photograph on page 220 by Charles Gibbons, courtesy of the United States Department of the Interior.

Also by Charles Kuralt

TO THE TOP OF THE WORLD:
The Adventures and Misadventures of
the Plaisted Polar Expedition

6

ANGEL'S CAMP, CALIFORNIA. The small towns are full of surprises. Who would guess that Angel's Camp, where Mark Twain once lived and worked, was named not for a heavenly angel, but for George Angel, an early settler, who, if he was like most early settlers around here, got along with neither wings nor halo?

"I have fallen in love with American names," Stephen Vincent Benét wrote, "the sharp names that never get fat; the snakeskin titles of mining claims; the plumed war bonnet of Medicine Hat, Tucson and Deadwood and Lost Mule Flat."

I know what Mr. Benét meant. I, too, have traveled through Gnaw Bone, Indiana, and Lizard Lick, North Carolina. I, too, have watched the sea break on Frying Pan Shoals and have passed the time of day with old-timers in Cripple Creek. The names and the towns and the people get into your bones and bloodstream.

Dateline America started on CBS Radio the first week of 1972. The broadcast resulted from the conviction of my employer, CBS News, that since I was out on the road anyway, finding television stories in places like Granny's Neck and Hell-For-Certain, and since I didn't have anything else to do, I might as well turn in a few radio essays on the weekends.

I didn't mind the added work. I had experienced many of the small inspirations and afterthoughts and irritations that come to any traveler; *Dateline America* was an opportunity to get them off my chest. Writing for radio is easier than for television; if you want to describe a sunset, you just describe it. You don't have to drag a heavy camera up a steep hill to prove how pretty it is. Besides, I was steeped in the Gospel According to Sevareid. Eric Sevareid, the best writer among broadcasters, always felt grumpy about television. One day he was heard to murmur, "One good word is worth a thousand pictures."

Mark Chester's good photographs for this book prove that Sevareid's rule doesn't hold true for all words and pictures, but another thing worries me a little bit. These words were meant to be heard, not read. I would appreciate it if you would supply your own background sounds—the gabble of the geese at Tule Lake, the clip-clop of the horse that pulls our carriage up the hill on Mackinac Island, the murmur of the breeze in the St. Martinville oaks.

I wrote these short pieces at my rattling desk on the bus I travel around in, or under sixty-watt light bulbs in motel rooms, or, willy-nilly, at the locations of stories. One I composed with the typewriter set up on a stump. They were recorded and shipped back to New York for broadcast or read into a microphone hooked to a telephone line. I have an idea that literature is not composed or transmitted in this manner, and I certify that the wary reader will find no literature lurking in these pages.

Mostly these are stories about moments of our past or about the small towns and ordinary people of our present—not the stuff of which most network radio is made. But if you leave such moments, places, and people out of the jigsaw puzzle of America, then you cannot see the country whole. That's probably another reason I spend so much time in places like Angel's Camp—to try to put in some of the missing pieces.

LOUISVILLE, KENTUCKY. As I was leaving a restaurant this week, I picked up a couple of matchbooks from the bowl on the counter.

"That will be five cents," said the lady at the cash register. I dropped those matchbooks back into the bowl as if they had ignited.

"Five cents!" I said. "For a couple of matchbooks? Look," I said, picking one up again gingerly, so as not to damage the merchandise, "they even advertise your restaurant. You are going to make me pay a nickel to go around advertising your restaurant? Look," I said, "they don't even tell the truth. See, right here it says, 'fine steaks.' "

"I am sorry, sir," she said, and I departed, leaving her lying matchbooks lying there.

I suppose matchbooks may be worth two for a nickel, considering that you can use them to level tables and to pick popcorn out of your teeth. It was just the shock of seeing matchbooks following road maps and after-dinner mints into the category of costly things that used to be free.

If you have to pay a nickel for two matchbooks, what good is a nickel any longer? I can remember when a nickel would buy a newspaper or a pencil or a Coke or a candy bar.

(Yes, child, there was a time when candy bars didn't cost twenty-nine cents.)

It wasn't so long ago that a nickel got you a ride on the Staten Island Ferry. Admittedly, after you spent your nickel, you found yourself in Staten Island, but for only another nickel you could get back again. Put another nickel in, in the nickelodeon. It's a quarterodeon now, and there aren't even any Jimmy Dorsey songs in it.

It is true that in the state of Louisiana you can still make a call from a pay phone for a nickel. But word has reached us that even now the phone company is trying to raise that to twenty cents because it needs $105 million right away. Nickels do make a difference to somebody, apparently, namely the phone company, which hates them unless they come in fours.

Well, go ahead, Louisiana, phase out the nickel phone call. All a nickel will buy then is two matchbooks—or a penny gumball.

BOONE, NORTH CAROLINA. Mountain people know a lot of things the rest of us have forgotten. It was a mild Christmas, and a mountain man told me today that means a heavy harvest next fall. I asked him if it always works out that way. He said he's never known it to fail.

On New Year's Day everybody in these mountains had black-eyed peas for dinner. If you did not, nobody back in these hollows would hold out much hope for your luck in the year to come. You probably also forgot to open your windows on the stroke of midnight New Year's Eve to let the bad luck out and the good luck in. All you can do now is hope to see a red-haired girl riding a white mule. That's good luck any time of year.

A farmer back in the hills remarked that he had to postpone hog killing this fall until the light of the moon. No mountaineer would any more kill hogs in the dark of the moon than he would dig potatoes. If you want to do something between the full moon and the new moon, why, of course, you must make soap or cut shingles.

Another thing mountain people know is that the first twelve days of January correspond to the first twelve months of the year when it comes to predicting weather. So if you want to know what the weather will be like in May, say, just look out the window on January 5.

There was snow on the ground in the shady patches this morning, melting slowly. "Waiting around for more," a woman said. She knows more snow is coming, and if the rooster crows at night, she knows it is coming before morning.

This week I visited a man with a considerable reputation as an

herb doctor. He asked me not to tell his name because he doesn't want to be caught practicing medicine without a license. There is really not much danger of that; even the sheriff's deputy comes to him for a remedy of wild-cherry bark juice mixed with corn whiskey. The herb doctor also finds, and prescribes, ginseng. Ginseng makes you live longer, he says, and because of its aphrodisiac qualities, makes living longer more fun. The first person to rave about ginseng, according to history, was a man named Shen Nung, and he didn't have to worry about being arrested for practicing medicine without a license because he gave out the licenses. Shen Nung was emperor of China in 3000 B.C. Shen Nung's secrets are still safe in the Blue Ridge.

Mountain people know so many things; it's a wonder those of us who don't know them can get along at all. If your nose itches, company is coming. If a honeybee buzzes around your head, you're about to find some money. Try to remember all this, will you? If you need to stop a cut from bleeding, just say the sixth verse of the sixteenth chapter of Ezekiel while walking toward the sunrise. Everybody around here knows that.

DUBUQUE, IOWA. I will never forget the first time I saw the black earth of Illinois. I was a boy from North Carolina, where the sky is bluer and richer, but where the dirt is redder and a whole lot poorer, and where a hundred acres is a big farm. Out here a hundred acres is hardly room enough to turn your combine around in. I knew midwestern farmers must be different, and sure enough, they are.

I think of those I've come to know:

The Wisconsin dairy farmer who pushes a button in his kitchen which activates a rotor that moves feed from his silo into his feed troughs to feed three hundred Holsteins at once while he has his breakfast coffee.

The Kansas wheat farmer who invited me to run into town with him. I thought he meant the town of Tribune, Kansas. When we got to the garage, there was no car; there was a plane. He meant Denver.

And then there's Bill Bodisch. We were tooling along through the snow near Bill Bodisch's place this week, with chains on the wheels of the bus that my friends and I use to wander the country, when suddenly we ran across a cattle guard. Links of those chains sprayed the surrounding countryside like machine-gun bullets at the battle of the Marne. With no chains, we were stuck in the snow. Pretty soon, here came Bill Bodisch on his tractor. He stopped and surveyed the damage. "Well, the problem is," he said, "your chains is busted up. They gotta be welded."

Visions of wreckers and machine shops and a bill for a hundred dollars and a five-hour wait in the snow! "May I use your phone?"

I said. "Well, no need to," he said. "Let me get 'em to the barn and I'll have 'em welded up in a jiffy."

While Bill was welding, a neighbor fired up one of his three Caterpillar tractors and pulled us up the hill to level ground. Back in North Carolina, see, we didn't have welding outfits and Caterpillar tractors. I mentioned this to Bill.

"Oh," he said, "you ain't seen nothin' yet." That was when he took us around behind the corncrib and showed us a little project of his. He's built it from scratch and he's just about finished. A fifty-eight-foot steel yacht. He hopes to head for the Mediterranean this spring.

Farming in the Middle West, as I say, is a little different.

NEW YORK CITY. I hardly ever cry, but next time I do, I'm ready. I can pull a handkerchief from my hip pocket big enough for a hippopotamus to weep into. It betrays my age, I suppose, that I never carry paper tissue. I believe in a healthy big square of cotton for drying crying eyes, blowing noses, mopping brows, mopping up spilled beer and ketchup stains, and offering to damsels in distress. It further betrays my age, I guess, that I carry around not only a handkerchief but also the out-of-date idea of damsels in distress. Damsels in distress these days use Dexedrine or karate chops to make themselves feel better and don't need handkerchiefs. But I still do. I carry one big enough to tie around my neck in dust storms. I haven't been in any dust storms lately, but I'd worry if I weren't prepared. A Kleenex tied around your neck in a dust storm would feel silly. And what if I severed an artery? That's the kind of thing I worry about —severing an artery with nothing to make a tourniquet out of but a Kleenex. I never venture out of the house without patting my hip pocket to make sure it's there, my big cotton handkerchief. Then I walk out into the morning, ready for dust storms and critical injuries.

Mary Knoblauch of the *Chicago Tribune* gave as her opinion once that the handkerchief is useful today merely as a status symbol. It symbolizes power, she said. If a man carries a handkerchief, it advertises to the world that he has the power to require someone to wash and iron it for him. Women, she says, who don't want to wash and iron handkerchiefs, were the first to give them up.

Maybe that's where the handkerchief went, the way of women's liberation. Well, I wash my own handkerchiefs, and nobody irons them, which is why they look a little scruffy sometimes. But just wait until Mary Knoblauch gets into a dust storm. Then she'll be looking around for me. And I hope I'm there. She'll be my first damsel in distress.

WATERBURY, CONNECTICUT. Everywhere you go around here, you can see piles of rubble that were, until this week, nice new buildings. It snowed a lot, and the roofs of the new buildings couldn't take it. You probably heard about the Hartford Civic Center, the pride of Connecticut. A few hours after thousands of people watched a basketball game, the roof came crashing down on the arena. One minute Hartford had a multimillion-dollar civic center, and the next minute it had a big pile of twisted structural steel.

But that wasn't the only roof that caved in. Day before yesterday, down the road here at Naugatuck, forty or fifty people were shopping in King's department store when ten thousand square feet of roof came down on them—nobody hurt seriously, but they all had a fright, and there was a lot of weeping and confusion for a while.

The night before, up in Milford, Massachusetts, the roof of the Value-King supermarket collapsed and six people were hurt. Josiah Birch, who works there, said he was stocking potatoes when he heard a sound like thunder, and down came the roof and filled the store with snow, an awful mess.

Some high school and college gyms have gone, besides, and some industrial buildings. A big garage on Main Street here in Waterbury caved in, and Michael Jones's garage down on Fiske Street, and I don't know how many other buildings, all of them relatively new, all designed along improved modern lines and built by the latest methods by up-to-date architects, engineers, and contractors. Along came a pretty good snowfall, and several dozen of these new buildings fell down.

Oh, by the way, not far from here I noticed a barn, an old New England barn, built, I would judge, 150 years ago—built of wood by a craftsman who knew what he was doing without benefit of computers. The snow also fell on that barn, and not just this snow but all the snows of the century. The barn roof is still there and isn't even sagging.

ARCOLA, ILLINOIS. The corn is as high as an elephant's eye in the grain belt this weekend, and on every back road you see trucks on their way to the corncribs heaped high with dry gold. Enough corn spills out on the curves to feed for a year the chickens that used to hang around the back porch of my youth.

The corn is so high that it blocks the view of Washington from here, but the farmers know that there are people in the State Department back there who think all this September bounty is good. Corn is our wealth and can be used as an instrument of foreign policy. No, says the Agriculture Department, corn is our poverty; farmers are growing too much of it for their own good and next year we'll have to cut back. A corn farmer who came into Arcola yesterday to buy a sack of cornmeal at an inflated price told me the whole thing has him confused.

The tobacco farmers back home in North Carolina are also harvesting and also confused. One branch of the government is handing out acreage allotments to keep them from going broke and on the dole—and another branch of the government is telling everybody that tobacco will kill you, in an effort to wipe out the tobacco crop completely.

It's tough to be a farmer these days, but no tougher than to be a highway worker. The government says you have to put warning beepers on your heavy equipment so you can hear when those big graders are backing up. And since road work is so noisy, the government also says you have to wear earplugs to protect your hearing. With earplugs, of course, you can't hear the warning beepers.

The government is trying to save the bobcat and ruled a few days ago that no more bobcat pelts can be exported. That's endangered-species protection. The government is also trying to kill the bobcat and hires trappers to do so. That's predator control.

I would just like to warn all those people in Washington that around Arcola, Illinois, the suspicion is growing that a government that cannot make up its mind about corn or tobacco or highway graders or bobcats may not be able to make up its mind about anything.

NEW YORK CITY. My father's folks came from Austria; where did your father's folks come from? From somewhere else, not here. Even if you're a full-blooded Cherokee, it's commonly accepted that your folks immigrated to America from somewhere else—on foot across the land bridge from Asia, maybe—and the rest of us got here in steerage from Liverpool or in tourist class from San Juan or in chains from the Ivory Coast.

They have opened Ellis Island to tourists, which means that the place where sixteen million strangers in fur hats and babushkas came knocking at the golden door may now be visited by their grandchildren wearing flowered shirts with cameras around their necks. It is an occasion for remembering that we all came from somewhere else.

We tend to forget. "Give me your tired, your poor . . ." were empty words to the Chinese and Japanese who were the first to be excluded, starting before the turn of the century. Then the Mexicans were shut out. Starting in 1917, you had to be able to read. Starting in 1920, quotas were set up for practically everybody. In 1924 the National Origins Act cut Italian immigration from the millions of the early years of the century to fewer than four thousand a year. John F. Kennedy said we should change that poem to read, "Give me your tired, your poor—as long as they come from northern Europe, are not retired or *too* poor, never stole a loaf of bread and never joined any questionable organization." It took us a long time, half a century and more, finally to change the law and polish the tarnish from the golden door.

That's because we forgot where we came from—somewhere else, not here. And we forgot who did the work of building America. Irish who came here expecting to be farmers ended up digging the Erie Canal. Italians who dreamed of starting orchards rooted out the New York subway system instead. Germans and Poles and Swedes and Chinese laid 350,000 miles of railroad track. Whole villages of Welsh came over to dig up Pennsylvania and fuel the insatiable engine of America. There were always more streets to pave, more water mains to build, and more waves of strong backs on the way across the oceans. New York, which had one million people in 1875, had 3.5 million in 1900, half of them foreign born. They lived in tenements that quite exceeded in hopelessness anything we call poverty today.

But *hopelessness* isn't quite the right word. Maybe hope is the one thing they did have, if not for themselves, then for their children. We are their children, and since we can't remember the flies, the crowding, the sickness, and the dirt, we ought at least to remember that people from somewhere else made this country for us.

28

GREAT SALT LAKE, UTAH. What's in the Great Salt Lake? Nothing, you say. Well, that's the wrong answer. I've just learned what's in the Great Salt Lake, and it's a rather long list. Number 1: Salt. Eight billion tons of salt, worth about fifty billion dollars. Also gypsum, magnesium, lithium, sulfur, boron, and potash. Number 2: Shrimp. Cute little shrimp, pink with big black eyes. Also flies, gnats, and algae. Number 3: People, mostly swimming people. Swimmers like the Great Salt Lake. Nonswimmers are absolutely knocked out by it because they can't sink. There is no record of anybody ever having gone swimming and drowned in the Great Salt Lake. The best life preserver, they say, is a ten-pound weight tied to your feet, to keep your feet down and your head up.

What else is in the Great Salt Lake? Number 4: A railroad. The solid rock-fill Southern Pacific trestle has divided the lake into two parts and two colors. The southern part is fresher and therefore bluer. Number 5: Waves. I met a man who said he was in a boat that was torn apart by Salt Lake waves. Waves on the lake are no bigger than anywhere else, but because they're so full of salt, they're heavier and pack a bigger wallop. Number 6: Islands. Several pretty islands, and *on* the islands, things like buffalo, jackrabbits, mountain lions, seagulls, coyotes, and pelicans. Number 7: Icebergs, in season. The lake doesn't freeze, but what happens is that fresh water from the rivers that feed the lake floats on top of the brine during calm weather, freezes, and gets piled up by the wind. Thirty years ago they spotted an iceberg thirty feet tall and half the size of a football field. Number 8: A monster. Or so it has been frequently testified. In 1877 a group of workmen swore a monster climbed out of the lake, bellowing, and chased them up a mountain. Number 9: Me. It's a hot day, and I'm about to go swimming, watching out for monsters. And that's what's in the Great Salt Lake.

CHESAPEAKE BAY, MARYLAND. We left the shore behind us this morning before dawn, and we were dredging the cold waters off Sharp's Rock as the sun came up. The crew members of the *Robert L. Webster* have spent every minute since on their knees beside the rail, laboriously separating bluepoints, one by one, from the rocks and mud and empty shells that the dredge also brings up. When we get fifty thousand oysters or so, we'll be able to go home.

This is hard, cold work. I couldn't do it for a day, but one of the *Robert L. Webster*'s crewmen has been at it for fifty years, and another for forty. This boat, this beautiful boat, is a member of the last fleet of working sailboats in the United States, the skipjacks. She was built in 1918 and set out on the Chesapeake in the fall of that year, dredging for oysters. She has dredged for oysters every autumn since. That is many autumns, but she'll not see another. Her captain, Eldon Willing, says he's going to tie the *Webster* up to the wharf when this season is over and get a construction job somewhere. The skipjack tradition is going and the skipjack fleet is dying a slow death on the Chesapeake.

It's not the hard work. Chesapeake watermen don't mind hard work. It's a combination of things, chiefly government regulations that seem to favor other, easier, more mechanical ways of taking oysters. Hydraulic tongs are a perfectly good way to do it, but they are not the skipjack's way. All the skipjacks are old, and nobody in his right mind would risk the cost of building a new one.

I have always admired them from shore. Captain Willing knows

I came out here to say good-bye but doesn't seem to resent me for it. He knows it is time to say good-bye to the leg-o'-mutton sloops with the clipper bows, good-bye to the lovely trail boards with the fine old names. *Caleb W. Jones, Seagull,* and *Lena Rose* are circling out here with us today, jibing their massive booms over the heads of crewmen working on their hands and knees like ours. The *City of Crisfield.* The *Rosy Parks.* The *Martha Lewis.* The *Ruby G. Ford.* They'll all be tied up to the wharf one day soon.

Captain Willing remembers when a thousand skipjacks worked the Chesapeake. Today there are thirty-two. Next year thirty-one—maybe fewer if other captains follow Eldon Willing ashore.

I wanted to say good-bye while I still could.

GARDEN CITY, KANSAS. I have memories of my grandfather's farm in North Carolina—two mules, one cow, no running water, no electricity. The most complicated piece of machinery on the farm was the hand water pump on the back porch.

Agriculture has come a long way since then. This week I stood in an automated barn watching cattle feed that was automatically balanced for fat and protein being mixed automatically by a computer to automatically feed twenty thousand head of perfectly nourished cattle that were waiting outside in the automated feed lot.

Just one thing: in the depths of the Depression, that one-man, one-cow farm in North Carolina fed a family. In these vastly more prosperous times, this space-age feed lot is feeding nothing but cattle. In fact, it is losing a lot of money.

All over the Great Plains, the screen doors of old homesteads are banging in the wind. The houses are empty; the farmers have sold out to their neighbors and moved to town. Only the big farms with much machinery and many hired hands and efficient planning can survive. Maybe even they can't survive. The American farming system, which is the envy of the world, is the despair of the American farmer.

There must be a way out. Jack Reeve, a cattleman, told me there is, but it is not a way we are going to like: it's higher and higher food costs.

"Fuel is up," Jack Reeve said. "Wages are up. Grain is up. Machinery costs about twice what it did five years ago. So that means people are just going to have to pay a lot more for what they eat. Every farmer and rancher around here is losing money. Some are losing a lot of money. Another year or two like this and there won't be any farmers or ranchers."

I admit I don't quite understand this. My grandfather's farm, which was small and primitive, and worked, has given way to agribusiness, which is large and computerized, and isn't working. An agricultural economist might be able to explain this to me. My grandfather probably could have explained it, but he is dead and gone, and where his farmhouse was, there is now a supermarket lot, where people park in order to pay four dollars a pound for Kansas beef.

ARCADIA, NEBRASKA. Now, this is the truth. A tornado blew through here last week, and the next day in a town seventy-five miles east, somebody picked up a canceled check that had been in an Arcadia businessman's desk drawer.

Impressed by this news, I turned to Roger Welsch, who teaches folklore at the university and keeps up with which way the Nebraska wind blows, to ask him if storms like that are common here.

Roger said he knew of a kid who was practicing on the tuba one day in Scottsbluff and a storm came along and screwed him twelve feet into the ground.

He said that after one of these Nebraska cyclones, a sleeping man found himself still in bed, but the bed was in the kitchen. The only damage done was that his underclothes were on upside down and buttoned in the back.

There was one Nebraska wind storm that twisted an eighteen-foot well over there in Howard County so bad that the bucket had to be drawn up with a corkscrew.

Another farmer had his chicken house blown away. After the wind subsided, he found that his only rooster had been blown into a half-gallon jug. He had to break the jug to get the rooster out and found the handle on the inside.

Barns back east have weather vanes on them to show which way the wind is blowing, but out here there's no need. Roger Welsch says farmers just look out the window to see which way the barn is leaning.

Some farmers, Roger says, attach a logging chain to a stout pole.

They can tell the wind direction by which way the chain is blowing. They don't worry about high wind until the chain starts whipping around and links begin snapping off. Then they know it's likely the wind will come up before morning.

LAKE TAHOE, CALIFORNIA. That irrepressible old tourist, Mark Twain, walked up the mountain from Carson City carrying an ax and a couple of blankets to take a look at Lake Tahoe and found it worth the climb.

"As it lay there," he wrote, "with the shadows of the mountains brilliantly photographed upon its still surface, I thought it must surely be the fairest picture the whole earth affords."

That was 115 years ago. Today there is smog about the lake.

"So singularly clear was the water," Mark Twain wrote, "that even where it was 80 feet deep, the bottom was perfectly distinct. . . . The water was not merely transparent, but dazzlingly, brilliantly so."

Today brown smudges muddy the water hundreds of yards out into the lake, the runoff from the towns on shore.

"Three miles away," Mark Twain wrote, "was a sawmill and some workmen, but there were not 15 other human beings throughout the wide circumference of the lake. . . . We did not see a human being but ourselves."

This afternoon fifteen people can be found at any crap table at Lake Tahoe. There is no such thing as solitude here, and never again will there be.

"We liked the appearance of the place," Mark Twain wrote, "and so we claimed some three hundred acres of it and stuck our notices on a tree. We were landowners now."

Here is an ad from this week's *San Francisco Chronicle:* "3.7

acres on Lake Tahoe, 4-bedroom house, 2-car garage, 200 feet lake frontage, $525,000."

Looking at what Lake Tahoe has become makes you want to turn back to Mark Twain for a glimpse of what it was.

"Lake Tahoe," he wrote, "would restore an Egyptian mummy to his pristine vigor and give him an appetite like an alligator. I do not mean the oldest and driest mummies, of course, but the fresher ones. The air up there in the clouds is very pure and fine, bracing and delicious. And why shouldn't it be?—it is the same the angels breathe."

Ah, Mark, the angels have moved. The condominium salesmen have taken their place.

JACKRABBIT, ARIZONA. I like Jackrabbit as a place, but especially as a name. Town names in Arizona have a realistic ring to them, probably because they were settled by realistic people. Oh, there are towns called Carefree and Friendly Corner and Eden in Arizona, even Inspiration and Paradise. And, of course, Phoenix. Chamber of Commerce names.

But most of those old settlers told it like it was, rough and rocky. They named their towns Rimrock, Rough Rock, Round Rock, and Wide Ruins, Skull Valley, Bitter Springs, Wolf Hole, Tombstone. It's a tough country. The names of Arizona towns tell you all you need to know.

Back east they name towns Willow Springs and Elmhurst and Appleville. Out here, where willows, elms, and apples will not grow, there's a town named Greasewood and another named Cuckelbur, and another named Hackberry. That's the honest truth, you see. Yucca, Arizona. It doesn't sound as pretty as Willow Springs, but it's the truth: no willows, lots of yucca.

Arizona settlers named some towns after their enemies—Cochise, Geronimo, Apache Junction, Navajo Station—and some after themselves—Lukeville, Jake's Corner, Lee's Ferry, Hannagan Meadow, Clint's Well, Happy Jack.

Few pale, effete, eastern names clutter the Arizona map. Arizonans favored boldness. In the last few days I have passed through Fort Apache, Fort Defiance, Two Guns, Dragoon, and Horse Thief Basin.

I don't know about you, but I am suspicious of Pleasantville, New

York. I am sure that Sawmill, Arizona, is more my kind of town. Or Window Rock or Hermits Rest or Turkey Flat or Grasshopper Junction. I could settle down here, just for the pleasure of having folks back home say, "Oh, don't you know what happened to old Charles? Lives now in Jackrabbit, Arizona. Just down the road from Cowlick and Bumble Bee."

NEWPORT, OREGON. In the second week of June, the coast of Oregon is alive as at no other time of year. I don't mean alive with people, although the weekend salmon fishermen are crowded into the bars and cafés along the bay front here in Newport. To see the kind of life I'm talking about, you have to leave town and drive down this magnificent coast along the cliffs and headlands. Golden splashes of scotch broom bank the road, improbably beautiful in the sun. The bright green coastal meadows are carpeted with daisies, and the fragile white flowers contrast with the sturdy dark trunks of towering Douglas fir, the spruce and hemlock, the myrtle and cedar. Everything that blooms is in bloom in the Oregon June: azaleas and rhododendron and, back at the edge of the forest, wild roses.

You look to the left and up to see all this. But if you do, you will be missing all the life that is to the right and down, below the cliffs at the edge of the sea. There are seals down there, and sea lions emerging from their caves to frolic in the surf, and seagulls and cormorants, and murre birds, which look like miniature flying penguins, skimming beyond the breakers. The sand crabs scuttle along the beach, the sculpins dart through the tidal pools, and otters roll in the coral sea.

In this season there is too much of life to see it all. To the south, inland from Pistol River, there is a wilderness area where the rarest of flowers grows, a kind of heath called *Kalmiopsis leachiania*. The Kalmiopsis is a living fossil, much studied. The visitor regarding with awe the burst of life and beauty in the second week of June, and wondering how many springs this has been going on, learns that the Kalmiopsis has been blooming now for 65 million years.

"Timeless beauty" is an expression that has meaning in June on the coast of Oregon.

WASHINGTON, D.C. Everybody knows there are too many lawyers in this country, but until now we've had to have them. We all carry around insurance policies, divorce decrees, and promissory notes written by lawyers, and from time to time it becomes necessary actually to *read* the damn things. Well, of course it can't be done. Only another lawyer can read what a lawyer has written. So you go to a lawyer. "What does this mean," you ask, "right here where it says, 'Each of the undersigned, together with any surety, guarantor, or any other party, hereto each hereby severally waives presentment hereof for payment, protest, and notice of protest, notice of dishonor, and all defenses by reason of any extension of time to its payment that may or shall be given by the holder or holders to them or any of them'? What does that mean?"

"Oh, that's simple," the lawyer says. "That just means that even if the bank gives you an extension of time to pay back the loan, you still have to pay it back."

The reason we have lawyers is the same reason we have Babylonian scholars. If something written in Babylonian happens to fall into your hands, you need somebody to read it to you.

This arrangement sends lawyers to bed each night feeling cozy and rich, but it may be about to end. Some banker down at the National Bank of Washington has decided to start writing loan forms in English instead of Babylonian. The new form actually says, for example, "Even if the bank gives me an extension of time to pay, I still must repay the loan."

That's all it really needs to say, and that's all it says. It doesn't take a lawyer to read it. Anybody can read it. No sureties, guarantors, or other parties, no hereofs, herebys, or heretos, no undersigned. Legalese, in this one place, has become a dead language, like Babylonian. This development has brought crowds of grateful speakers of English to borrow money from the National Bank of Washington. If it catches on, it will send hordes of lawyers into employment offices seeking honest work.

MOBILE, ALABAMA. Travel is broadening, as Marco Polo observed while trying to lose the thirty pounds he gained from all that chow mein, and you can't stay on the road constantly, as I do, without learning a thing or two along the way.

One: Never sleep on the side of the motel bed next to the telephone table. That's where you're inclined to sleep, on the grounds that it will be easier to answer your wake-up call in the gray dawn. Ah, but that's what every milk-fed, corn-fattened, 250-pound traveling salesman from Dubuque figures, too. That's where he sleeps, and that's where he sits to make his phone calls to the home office, so the side of the mattress next to the telephone table is broken down, and you spend the night at a perilous angle, your slumber lost to the necessity of keeping a tight grip on the uphill sheets to keep from falling onto the floor. One motel in ten puts the phone on a desk. That's nice. One motel in fifty turns the mattress occasionally. That's even nicer. In all others, sleep as far from the phone as possible.

Two: If you don't like loud rock music, change the settings on the rental car radio as soon as you rent it. The guys who park rental cars all like rock music, and the push buttons of all rental car radios are set for rock stations. Sometimes *all* the buttons are set for the *same* rock station. Once I turned in a rental car with the buttons soothingly set to pretty music, or at least innocuous music, and found it necessary, because of a change in plans, to rerent the same car ten minutes later. I am still shaking from the jolt to my psyche. Every button had already been changed to hard rock. It doesn't take 'em long.

Three: Don't always assume that the man in uniform in the

hotel lobby is the bell captain. A friend of mine did so recently in Annapolis, breezily ordering the guy with all the gold braid and the black bow tie to take the bags upstairs. I cannot repeat the rejoinder on a family network. The bell captain was a navy commander in full formal regalia. The navy really ought to keep commanders who are going to dances from hanging around hotel lobbies.

Four: If you rub a thin film of soap on the bathroom mirror before showering, it will keep the mirror from steaming up.

Five: If you leave your "Do Not Disturb" sign on the door and your television set turned on when you go out to dinner, it might prevent the night maid's boyfriend from stealing your suit. (It might not.)

Six: If you have heavy packages to carry from the plane and a mile of airport corridors to negotiate, carry a bandage in your pocket for wrapping around your ankle and affect a limp. They will call you a wheelchair.

These musings may sound cynical, but travel not only broadens, it jangles the nerves, as every traveler knows. Saint Paul, who traveled a bit himself, wrote in Second Corinthians, "Thrice I have suffered shipwreck, a night and a day I have been in the deep, in journeyings often, in perils of waters, in perils of robbers, in perils by mine own countrymen and by the heathen, in the city and the wilderness and the sea . . . in weariness and painfulness and cold."

I know, I know. And Saint Paul didn't even have to worry about the push buttons on Hertz cars.

OKEFENOKEE SWAMP, GEORGIA. This is where the cooters and the crackers get along together just fine. The cooters are the terrapins who stick their heads up out of the tannin-stained brown water. The crackers are the folks, the good people who live on the margins of the Okefenokee. I don't know of any place where human beings coexist so happily with God's other creatures.

It wasn't always so. Real estate speculators tried to drain the beautiful big swamp once. The swamp beat them. Lumber speculators once tried to cut down all the cypress trees, but by the grace of God and the tangled thicket of the Okefenokee, it cost them more than it paid, so they stopped. If you can't beat a swamp, join it, and that's what people around here have done now. They're proud of the Okefenokee, proud of its impenetrable places, proud that nobody quite knows whether there are still bears and panthers and ivory-billed woodpeckers living deep in the Okefenokee. There are places in there where nobody can go to find out.

Naturalists have Latin names for all the abundance of plants and animals that live here, I suppose, but I like the local names. Neverwets and floating hearts, spatterdocks and maiden cane—those are plants. Thunderpumps—those are bitterns. Cham-chacks—those are red-headed woodpeckers. "There's a good god sitting in the hoo-raws," a swamp man will say. That's a pileated woodpecker in a bush. I used to know a man down here named John Holt who rode around the swamps in a johnboat, eating King Edward cigars and admiring the scenery. One day we saw the head of an alligator resting on a log. "There's a 'gator's head," John said, as he chewed up

another cigar. As we approached, the alligator heaved himself over the log and slid into the water. He was a giant. John Holt said, "Did you notice how much 'gator there was following that head? That's why we have so many peg-legged men around here."

He was just kidding. The 'gators leave the folks alone and vice versa. The Okefenokee is a happy place for 'gators and tree frogs and herons and mud turtles and sandhill cranes and cooters and crackers —an excellent argument for not paving quite everything.

SALMON, IDAHO. People pass through this valley, intent on the lovely Rocky Mountain scenery, without knowing that anything important ever happened here. What happened here is, to me, one of the most dramatic and romantic and disappointing stories in the whole, long march of human history.

Late in the summer of 1805, two young Virginians, Meriwether Lewis and William Clark, climbed over the Continental Divide just east of here and made their way down to the Salmon River. They were the first white men ever to see what is now Idaho. Their friend Thomas Jefferson, who had sent them here, was sure they would find a water route to the Pacific, and when Lewis and Clark set eyes on the Salmon River, they thought they had found it. Quite excited, Clark went ahead to reconnoiter. He walked around a bend of the broad, smooth-flowing Salmon, and his heart sank.

"The river," he wrote in his journal, "becomes almost one continued rapid. The mountains close . . . a perpendicular cliff on each side . . . the water runs with great violence from one rock to another, foaming and roaring through the rocks in every direction. The passage with canoes is entirely impossible."

It turned out that the Salmon River was merely an irritation to Lewis and Clark. It meant they had to negotiate with the Shoshone Indians for horses in order to continue their march of discovery. It meant they had to abandon the canoes they had used all the way from the Mississippi.

But to the rest of the world, the news they brought back from here was shattering. It meant that the earnest belief of three hundred years was wrong. It meant that you could not reach the Pacific coast and Asia by following the waterways west. It meant that there was no Northwest Passage. The dream of Columbus ended here, at the first rapids of the Salmon River.

Stand here and you can feel more than the spray of a great and turbulent river. You can feel the disappointment of the ages.

ELMSFORD, NEW YORK. They've turned the old railroad depot here into an antique shop, which is better than turning it into a parking lot. The railroad depots shaped our history. We built forty thousand of them in the small towns and great cities, one-room village depots with projecting eaves and pot-bellied stoves, and baroque palaces like Grand Central Station. We have torn down more than half of them already, and we can't afford to lose very many more.

Elmsford is lucky to have kept its depot and to have gained an antique shop in the bargain. A newspaper office has taken over the terminal at Waterbury, Connecticut. In Byars, Oklahoma, the former station is a church. The magnificent old terminal in Chattanooga has become the restaurant of the Choo Choo Hilton. The Choo Choo is a little chi-chi, but it's better than the wrecking ball.

In many a town the railroad station that is now ignored, boarded up, was once the center of everything. The stationmaster was an important man since all the big news from outside reached him first, by telegraph. The depot was the place from which the young set off for the big cities to seek their fortunes and the place which those coming home strained to catch a glimpse of as the train slowed down at the yard limit. We bulldoze such buildings at the peril of forgetting who we were. Turning them into boutiques or discos is one way to save them.

My friend Oliver Jensen had an even better idea. He found that the best way to save the old station at Essex, Connecticut, was to charter a railroad. So he did. He gives people rides up the Connecticut River, and he has turned the railroad depot into a railroad depot.

MILLE LACS, MINNESOTA. I made the mistake of looking at the thermometer before venturing out of the cabin I was staying in a few days ago. The thermometer read thirty-eight degrees below zero. I put on my quilted goose-down thermal underwear, two or three heavy sweaters, my arctic explorer's britches, my fur-lined parka, my ski mask, my stocking cap, my snowmobile boots, and my mittens and lumbered outside, where I ran into Art Heggedahl. He was wearing a shirt open at the neck and work pants and sneakers. "It's cold," I said. "Yeah," he said. "If it gets any colder, I'm going to have to get myself a hat."

Minnesotans are just different, that's all. On the day of which I speak, with the wind-chill factor hovering at fifty-seven below, hundreds of them could be perceived through the slits in my ski mask out ice fishing on this frozen lake. It was cold out there, bitter, biting, cutting, piercing, hyperborean, marmoreal cold, and there were all these Minnesotans running around outdoors, happy as lambs in the spring.

I don't know how to explain it, unless it is a kind of gelidity in the blood, inherited from the generations of deep-frozen Norwegians, Finns, and Swedes from whom most Minnesotans come, chips off the old icebergs.

Or maybe they stay drunk all winter. It did not escape my notice that brandy sells around here like Dr. Pepper in Dalton, Georgia. If you drink enough of the stuff, I suppose you don't notice the cold until your toes start falling off and rattling around in your boots.

Or maybe they really are cold and don't want to admit it to a

visiting southerner for fear of somehow besmirching the pride of the state, which calls itself the Star of the North.

Whatever the explanation, Minnesotans can take it. The state seal shows a farmer, a waterfall, a forest, and an Indian riding into the sunset. It should be changed to ice cubes rampant on a field of white, a grinning, barefoot Swede in a Grain Belt Beer T-shirt riding a snowmobile, and a shivering visitor whose stricken breath is freezing into ice crystals. The model for the latter could be your humble, frostbitten servant, except that I'm getting out of here. A case of cold feet.

INDEPENDENCE ROCK, WYOMING. This rock was an invitation no passerby could resist. It bulges up from the desert right beside the Oregon Trail, and it begs to be written upon. And so they wrote upon it, and some of them did such a careful job with hammer and chisel that their names are still plainly visible: "Milo J. Ayer, age 29, 1849." He had heard about gold in California, no doubt. You stand here and look at the neatly carved name of a forty-niner, Milo J. Ayer, and the anonymity of the Gold Rush falls away. You want to know more. Did you make it to California, Milo, and if so, how did you fare with your pick and your pan? Nothing at Independence Rock testifies to that. All it says is "Milo J. Ayer, age 29, 1849."

There are hundreds of other names written large on the big rocks along the Oregon Trail. Each invests the abstract facts of American history, the westward migration, Manifest Destiny, with a fragment of humanity. These were not just pioneers; these were people, with names: "Jedediah Hines," it says on the steep stone face called Register Cliff. And ages: "J. R. Hornaday, aged 19 yrs., 1 month, 9 days." And hometowns: "Samuel White, Phoenixville, Pennsylvania." "Fox, Cincinnati, Ohio." "Ryan, Indianapolis."

It was graffiti when it was written. But it is history now, very personal and affecting history. The first sixty-nine people plodded these two thousand miles from Missouri to Oregon in 1841. Two hundred people the year after that. A thousand the year after that. In places the Oregon Trail is a lonely wagon track through the sagebrush. But in other places it is Interstate 25, and more people pass

along it in an hour than passed in those first three years. It is all so easy for us.

It wasn't easy for them. There is a grave on the average of every eighty yards along the Oregon Trail from Independence, Missouri, to the Continental Divide. Accidents, Indian attacks, cholera, and typhoid accounted for twenty thousand lives along this hellish track in less than thirty years. The graves are mostly unmarked. Only the living left their names in Wyoming.

If you make your way along a rough bank below Register Cliff and push aside some young cottonwoods that have grown up there, your reward is a political sentiment of 1861 carved in a large and enthusiastic script: "Hurrah For Old Abe And The Union!"

That patriot was the only pioneer I could find in a couple of days of perusing the name-bearing rocks who yielded up any of his thoughts. The others put down their names and where they had come from and little else. It was a way of saying, "You see, I have made it this far, all the way from Maryville, Missouri. Think of that!"

Yes, think of that.

SUN CITY, ARIZONA. By the middle of the day, the women's and men's choruses will have already finished their rehearsals in time for the men to get to one of the nine golf courses and for the women to make it to the tennis courts, the stitchers' workshop, or the art class. The defensive driving class had to be over by noon because some of its members are in the Pinochle Club, which meets at one o'clock. Open sewing ends early today because everybody has to go home and get ready for the Dance Club ball tonight. Everybody who lives here in Sun City is old and worn out and retired, you see, so they have plenty of time for all this. Many of them get up at six o'clock in the morning, before the activities start, to get in some jogging, biking, or swimming.

Sometimes there are conflicts. Yesterday ceramics conflicted with the ladies' gym class, both at eight-thirty in the morning. At nine, the art workshop coincided with the hand-bell ringers' rehearsal. But usually the old folks can work things out by skipping lunch. The Chess Club, for example, went right through from twelve to three-thirty yesterday, letting out in time for the Camera Club meeting, and the lawn-bowling meet wasn't until seven, so that was fine. The Organ Club, the Puppet Club, the Whist, Euchre, and Cribbage clubs, the Rock and Gem Club, and the Railroad Club had to squeeze in their meetings whenever they could.

Of course, some of the club members couldn't make it at all yesterday. This *is* a retirement community, after all, and you can't expect old folks to have the energy they once had. Some of them were just taking it easy down at the garden of the Agricultural Club or out on the horse trails or down at the skeet-shooting range. A few were shooting pool—pocket, snooker, or three-cushion—and the eyes go when you get old, you know, so the side bets are usually just moderate ones. And then after a game of pool, it's usual to rest up with just a little boating or bowling or square dancing, and then taper off toward evening at a meeting of the Leathercrafters, Silvercrafters, or Bicycle Club or maybe a quiet game of tennis—usually doubles, which is easier than singles for old, worn-out, retired folks.

MADISON, WISCONSIN. I complained in public the other day that football cheers are neither as lusty nor as silly as they used to be. This has brought me the recollection of a lot of silly cheers of days gone by. These are all dead cheers, I believe, as moribund in academe as puns in Latin.

Mr. W. L. Fleming of Boise regrets the passing of the Idaho Potato Cheer:

> Dice 'em, hash 'em, boil 'em, mash 'em!
> Idaho, Idaho, Idaho!

Mr. James E. Carter, formerly of the University of Oregon, remembers cheering:

> Kick 'em up a gum tree, slide 'em down a cactus,
> We think Idaho needs more practice!

If you can imagine tens of thousands of football fans on opposite sides of the field shouting these old favorites at each other, you begin to see what society has lost.

I thought the famous technical cheer of Cal Tech was the most erudite of cheers:

> Secant, cosine, tangent, sine,
> Logarithm, logarithm, hyperbolic sine,
> Three-point-1-4-1-5-9,
> Slip stick, slide rule, Tech, Tech, Tech!

But I have been corrected by my erudite friend Mr. Emerson Stone, who says quite rightly, and eruditely, that this honor must go to the Yale cheer:

> Brek-ek-ek-ek! Co-ax! Co-ax!

It doesn't *sound* very erudite until you know, as every Yale student knows, that it is derived from the croaking chorus in *The Frogs* by Aristophanes. Only in the Ivy League does Aristophanes strike fear into the hearts of opposing football teams.

I suspect that this generation of laid-back students would be a little diffident about cheering the real cheers, like the one that Mr. T. E. Foreman used to cheer at Dawson County High in Glendive, Montana, forty-five years ago:

> With a veevo, with a vivo,
> With a veevo-vivo-vum,
> Boom, get a rat trap, bigger than a cat trap,
> Boom, get another one, bigger than the other one,
> Nikolater, whole potater,
> Half past alligator,
> Rim ram bulligator, chickalala,
> Dawson County High School, rah, rah, rah!

You're right, Mr. Foreman, that's a silly cheer.

Pat Harmon, sports editor of the *Cincinnati Post,* says his wife, Anne, remembers that the conventional cheer of Neoga High in Illinois went:

> Red and white, fight, fight, fight!

But in her senior year they got fancy on the colors and changed it to:

> Scarlet and platinum, come on, let's flatten 'em!

Robert B. Shepard of San Diego sends in the following disgusting entry from Eagle, Nebraska, High, circa 1916:

Chew tobacco, chew tobacco,
Chew tobacco, SPIT!
Eagle High School,
We are IT!

He says they also sang, to the tune of "My Country, 'Tis of Thee":

There ain't no flies on us,
There ain't no flies on us,
No flies on us.
There may be one or two
Great big green flies on you,
There ain't no flies on us,
No flies on us!

I opened one letter with no salutation and no signature. All it said was:

Found a raindrop, found a raindrop,
Found a raindrop in the sky.
But I'd rather be a raindrop
Than a drip from Tully High!

That's an old one, I imagine, but one letter pointed out that cheers don't have to be so old to be silly. Jon Schwenzer, who attended my old school, North Carolina, in the sixties, says that in that recent and sometimes silly decade they used to cheer:

Marijuana, marijuana, Ho Chi Minh,
Come on, Tar Heels, first and ten!

HOLLYWOOD, CALIFORNIA. We had a beef shortage for a while there and survived it. When the gas shortage came along, we knew it would end eventually. But the collar button shortage looks permanent.

I have spent my week crossing the country and looking, in the meantime, for a collar button and studs for a formal shirt. For the benefit of the young among us, a proper formal shirt cannot be worn, or even buttoned, without studs and a collar button. I had an invitation to an awards ceremony, and the invitation said, "Black Tie." So I needed shirt studs and a collar button. The last time I noticed, they sold shirt studs and collar buttons in every hat shop.

Well, there are no more hat shops and no more collar buttons. Bloomingdale's in New York, which has everything, does not have collar buttons. Neither does Gimbel's in Pittsburgh. Neither do half a dozen men's stores in Dallas.

I didn't win any awards at the awards ceremony, which is just as well, because if I had, I'd have been forced to stand up there where everybody could see that my formal shirt was being held together by paper clips. When I asked for shirt studs in Hollywood the day of the dinner, everybody giggled at me. One store had one set, discovered in a bottom drawer. I had to decline them. They were silver sunbursts with rhinestones, each the size of a half-dollar.

And by the way, whatever happened to half-dollars? And bicycles, the kind with fat tires and no gears? Whatever happened to opera glasses?

I'll tell you what happened; the same thing that happened to ink.

I spent a long day in Miami several years ago looking for a bottle of ink. Woolworth's, for heaven's sake, said no ink. Sears said they could order it. A fountain pen without ink is like a formal shirt without a collar button.

Whatever happened to milkshakes—real milkshakes, I mean? Whatever happened to canning jars? Have you tried to buy any canning jars lately?

I don't think we can blame this on the Arabs. I think it's more sinister than that. I think somebody has decided we will no longer dress formally, write with fountain pens, drink real milkshakes, or can peaches the way we used to—that blue jeans and ballpoints are good enough for us, that those execrable soft ice cream milkshakes and those syrupy sweet canned peaches will do. Well, they won't do, but what can we do about it?

Whatever happened to 78-rpm records and convertible cars? Whatever happened to photo corners, which you used to mount pictures of pinup girls? Whatever happened to pinup girls? What's going on around here?

DODGE CITY, KANSAS. Mr. Willis Grumbein of Dodge City recently spoke to us on the public airwaves about mules, which he sells. Oh, the wonder of mules, he said. They are not stubborn, they work with a will, never kick you unless you need it, and never stray far from home.

Much mail has followed. A citizen of Wilkes County, North Carolina, says his mule kicked him and broke his shoulder the day before Willis Grumbein praised mules on the air.

A Harvard professor, and former mule owner, says every one of his mules broke through a fence one time and strayed as far as twelve miles, causing him to have to chase them all the night and most of the next day.

A man from Alabama, who seems to know mules, sent me a quotation from Josh Billings: "I've known mules to be good for six months so as to get a chance to kick."

The general attorney of the Carolina Power and Light Company sent me a long legal answer once filed by his company in response to a lawsuit from a man whose mule had been electrocuted by a neighbor's electric fence. "It is in the nature of mules," this legal document asserted, "to be restive under restraint, to slip bridles, halters or other instrumentalities with which they may be tethered, and in the exercise of freedom thus gained, to wander from their owner's estates to that of others." "A mule," the company said to the court, "being the hybrid result of the cross of a horse with an ass, is trusted least by those who know him best, since he sometimes

behaves like an ass's horse, and sometimes like a horse's ass, for all of which, indeed, he is both."

Somebody from West Virginia sent me one of Jim Comstock's mule stories. The editor of the *West Virginia Hillbilly* wrote one time that when Punk Green's mother-in-law was kicked to death by a mule, the wake was so crowded people could hardly find a place to sit and sing. A fellow said, "Punk, your mother-in-law must have been mighty popular."

Punk said, "Well, actually they didn't come to the funeral. They come to buy that old mule."

SALVO, NORTH CAROLINA. It is winter on the Outer Banks. At this time of year you can walk nearly one hundred miles down the wild barrier beaches without meeting another living soul. Hunch your back against the wind, put your hands in your pockets, and ponder, as you walk, the mystery of the first Europeans to know this coast.

They came in 1587 from England, the noble England of Elizabeth and Shakespeare and Francis Drake. They settled on a safe island, Roanoke, protected from the sea by this sand barrier we are walking on. The site was that of an earlier settlement that had given up a couple of years earlier and gone home to England. These people meant to stay, to establish, under Sir Walter Raleigh's patronage, an English claim to the new continent.

We know their names—Christopher Cooper and John Bright and William Waters and Jane Jones and Margaret Lawrence and Rose Payne—names so much like our own. We know how they lived —in thatched-roof cottages in a kind of English village. We know about the birth, that first summer, of the first English child in the new world—the daughter of Eleanor and Ananias Dare, named Virginia.

We know everything about those first colonists except what happened to them.

Their governor, John White, went home to England after a year to bring back supplies. He wasn't able to return on schedule because of the outbreak of war with Spain. When he did come back, three years later, full of anxiety, he found the village deserted. A single

word was carved on a tree, the word *Croatoan,* the name of a nearby Indian village.

Were the settlers massacred by the Croatoans? Or did they move to the Croatoan village for protection against more warlike Indians, intermarry, and become the forebears of a blue-eyed Indian tribe, the Lumbees, which still exists? Or did they try to return to England and lose their lives at sea? Or were they discovered by Spaniards from Florida and taken away as captives?

We do not know. We will never know.

We owe so much to that English colony. They brought English names and English speech and English laws to this continent. We ought to put up a monument to them. If only we knew where to put it.

CINCINNATI, OHIO. This is going to get me into a lot of trouble, so I'd better say at the start that I *like* trucks. I like pickup trucks, flatbed trucks, cattle trucks, delivery trucks, moving trucks, and garbage trucks. And I like truck drivers. I am one myself, if you can call a battered twenty-six-foot CBS motor home a truck. It takes a heap o' livin' to make a home a truck, but I have been out here on the road for more than ten years now, and I was beginning to feel brotherly toward the big boys. I know you have to have the patience of Job and a belly of cast iron to push those eighteen-wheelers from Oakland to Hoboken. I know all that, and I still say something's got to be done about trucks.

Every time I look in my rearview mirror these days, it's filled up by the grille of a big Mack diesel. Ever since the fifty-five-mile-an-hour speed limit came in, trucks have been following too close. If, as a driver, you are stubborn about obeying the law, you get the tailgating treatment and then you get the air horn—meaning get over in the left lane, you idiot, so I can pass you on the right. There are about 260,000 heavy-duty, long-haul trucks on the road, and every one of them has passed me on the right going seventy. It is intimidating in good weather and terrifying in bad. I am not talking about an occasional truck. Nearly all trucks, as far as I can figure out, follow too close, drive too fast, and cut in too quickly after passing, often before their tailgates pass your front bumper. I have frequently had to go to the brakes to avoid going into the guard rail.

We used to think of truckers as knights of the road, always stopping to change the tires of elderly widows. Now, with their CB

radios giving them warning of police radar, and the interstate highways sparing them from the necessity of ever shifting down from
thirteenth gear, the knights have become bullies. Though they break
the law all day and all night, I don't remember ever seeing a truck
stopped by a highway patrolman. Maybe the cops are as frightened
of trucks as I am.

JONESBORO, ARKANSAS. We are importing, I read in the paper, millions of tons of oil. How much oil is *that?* I asked myself; so I called my friend the expert.

"How many barrels in a ton?" I inquired.

"Gross ton or net ton?" he said.

"I don't know," I said.

"Well," he said, "I mean long ton or short ton?"

"I don't know," I said.

"Metric ton, avoirdupois ton, or troy ton?" he asked.

"Look," I said, "stop showing off. All I want to know is how many barrels in a ton."

"Well," he said, "maybe we'd better start at the beginning. How many gallons are in this barrel you're talking about?"

"What difference does it make?" I asked. "How many gallons are in any barrel?"

"Well," he said, "31 gallons if it's wine or beer. Thirty-one and a half if it's water, including rain water, except in four states where rain barrels are by law larger than beer barrels. If there's whiskey in the barrel, under federal law the barrel holds exactly 40 gallons. If the barrel holds fruit or vegetables, it's 105 dry quarts."

"A hundred and five dry quarts," I said.

"Yes," the expert said, "except cranberries."

"Cranberries," I said.

"Yes," he said, "a cranberry barrel is only 86 and 45/64ths dry quarts, of course."

"Of course," I said. "Well, there's oil in the barrel."

"Refined oil or crude oil?" he asked.

"Crude oil," I said.

"What kind of gallons?" he asked.

"What do you mean what kind of gallons?" I shouted.

"U.S. Standard or British Imperial?" he asked.

"Gallons, gallons, the kind you put in a car!" I said.

"You must mean the United States gallon of 128 United States fluid ounces," he said patiently. "The British gallon is different, namely, the volume of 10 pounds of water at a temperature of 62 degrees Fahrenheit. Both pounds and Fahrenheit are on the way out, of course, as are gallons and barrels. The metric system will be much simpler. A meter, for example, is simply one million, 650 thousand, 763-point-73 wavelengths in vacuum of the orange-red line of the spectrum of the element Krypton-86 . . ."

I interrupted him. "Look," I said, "I'm just trying to figure out how much oil we're importing."

"Oh," he said, "heaps."

JASPER, TEXAS. This is a story told by east Texas domino players. They swear it is true, but then an east Texas domino player will swear to anything. If you know Jasper or Woodville or Livingston or any of the other county seats around here, you know that the domino player's day begins late in the morning under the old oak trees in the courthouse square and ends when it begins to get cool in the afternoon and it's time to milk the cow or whatever else domino players do when they are not playing dominos and lying to each other. That leaves time for a lot of lying.

Anyway, they *say* it's true that last winter one of those little fly-by-night carnivals came down the road from a show in Lufkin, on its way to a show in Splendora, and right there on Highway 59 the carnival experienced a tragedy. Its baboon died. There wasn't time for a decent burial, so they just left the dead baboon beside the road and went on.

Well, some of the boys coming home from duck hunting in their pickup truck saw the carcass, stopped, backed up, and fell to arguing about what it was. They couldn't agree, so they concluded they'd put the creature in the back of the pickup and take him down to Doc Milam for purposes of identification. Doc Milam is the wisest man in the county when it comes to animals, with a lively practice in colicky horses and cattle who are off their feed, and it wasn't long before the dead baboon was laid out on his back porch, with the boys crowding around to hear Doc Milam's verdict.

Doc came out on the porch and looked over the top of his spectacles at the baboon, and bent over and took a closer look, and scratched his head for a minute. Then he said, "Well, I've never seen one just like him before . . ." The boys crowded in closer.

"But," Doc Milam said, "it's easy to see what he is. He's got those bulging eyes, and those long fingernails, and the shaggy hair, and his bottom is rubbed right raw. There's only one thing he could be."

"What's that?" one of the boys asked.

"Well," Doc Milam said, "I would say that what we have here is an old east Texas domino player."

BOSTON. During the Revolution, people in Boston used to say, Sam Adams did the writing and John Hancock paid the postage. Brilliant Sam Adams and his wealthy friend Hancock were among the targets of the march of the Redcoats to Lexington and Concord. They were to be captured and tried for treason, of which they were unmistakably guilty. But they escaped and lived to see their country free. They are buried not far from each other in the same cemetery, a few steps from Boston Common. Robert Treat Paine, who also signed the Declaration of Independence, and James Otis, the fiery patriot who survived the Revolution only to be killed by lightning, lie in this same, small, tree-shaded place, the Old Granary Burying Ground. So does the black man Crispus Attucks and the others who were shot down by British soldiers in the Boston Massacre.

There are some patriots buried here of whom you may not have heard. One gravestone says, "Elisha Brown. He bravely and successfully opposed a whole British regiment in their violent attempt to force him from his legal habitation."

He *did*? Why, this Elisha Brown must have been quite a man! It turns out Elisha did it by buying a lot of groceries. When the British occupied Boston in 1769 and forced every householder to give food and shelter to the troops, Elisha Brown decided he wouldn't. He put in enough food for a year, barred his doors, locked his windows, and settled down for a long stay. His food held out longer than British patience. After a few weeks they marked him down as a stubborn old fool and went away and left him alone.

This old graveyard is full of stubborn men. This one, a stone says, "was wounded by the enemy and died painfully of his wounds." This one died "opposing the British." It doesn't say how this man died, but we remember his name, and how stubborn Paul Revere was.

If you come to Boston, leave the busy street for a few minutes and walk into this quiet place. It's a good place to think.

The thought that crossed my mind was that all these men were neighbors. What a neighborhood!

DORRANCE, KANSAS. I stopped by to see a farmer near here the other day, walked up to the front door and knocked. No answer, no sign of life. I walked around to the back door and knocked. He came to the door right away and asked me into the kitchen, where were seated his wife, his son and daughter-in-law, and two grandchildren. Not one of them had heard the knock on the front door, and thinking about it later, I realized it was because they weren't used to listening for knocks at the front door. Nobody ever knocks at the front door. All through the South and up into the Great Plains, front doors stand locked and unused. I don't know anybody on any farm in America who uses the front door ever, except for funerals.

Now comes a letter from my friend Roger Welsch, professor of English and anthropology at the University of Nebraska and student of difficult questions, with an explanation. People *used* to use front doors, he says, before the turn of the century. But then things got informal. Everybody started using first names, formal dress and formal dining faded to the status of comedy, and people started opening up their kitchens to strangers. Hardly a person now living in rural America can remember using the front door. Many front doors don't even have steps up to them anymore. There is a kind of *memory* of the front door: when you use the back door, Roger Welsch points out, the woman of the house always says, "Oh, excuse the mess out there on the porch, the men just came in from the fields, the kitchen is such a mess because, you know, I'm right in the middle of cooking . . ." But just the same, if you knock on the front door, nobody will come, because nobody will hear. You are expected at the back. The front door leads to a parlor that was built in the time, or at least with the ancestral memory, of formality. But formality is all gone in America, and the parlors are unheated and unused, like the locked front doors that lead to them. What we've got here—everywhere outside the cities—is a back-door society. Roger Welsch says he asked somebody on a Nebraska farm about the abandoned front door and was told, "Oh, good heavens, if somebody comes to the front door, the dogs go crazy and the kids hide under the bed."

GOODLAND, KANSAS. The summer motorist, headed west, would be well advised to stock up on peanut butter sandwiches before leaving Kansas City, for there is nothing to eat until one reaches Denver. Kansas is the gastronomic wasteland of America. Save only Gordon Butte's hotel dining room in the cowtown of Alma, there is not, so far as I have been able to tell, a real restaurant in the state.

This is the home of the limp french fry, the 3.2 beer, the soft ice cream cone, and the chicken-fried steak. It is also the home of Carrie Nation, whose relentless opinions about alcohol so relentlessly prevail half a century after her death that only rarely in Kansas can you even have a drink to help you overlook what you are about to eat.

Fatted calves abound in Kansas. You can see them from Interstate 70. Heaven knows in what far-flung restaurants all this handsome beef winds up. Heaven also knows, not around here. This is the time of the wheat harvest, and combines clatter across the plain. This wheat probably will make very good bread in Russia. Kansas's idea of bread is the hot dog bun. Much good food is here, on the hoof and on the stalk, but not on the table. Water, water everywhere, and not a drop to drink

I don't know how a people so pleasant as Kansans ever grew so indifferent about food. Cardboard hamburgers that are laughed at elsewhere apparently are all shipped into Kansas as seconds. They sell like mad to big-boned teen-agers who, never having tasted real food, know no better.

No doubt, some very good cooking goes on in Kansas farmhouse kitchens while strangers starve. Come to think of it, one of the best meals I ever had came off the stove of Doretta Hoffman in the Kansas town of Manhattan. She was dean of home economics at Kansas State. All her students must have gone elsewhere upon graduation.

Before you cross the Missouri River, pack a lunch.

ELY, MINNESOTA. A splendid wilderness lies just outside town, thousands of blue lakes connected by a lacework of bright streams, ringed by pine and balsam and birch. The Boundary Waters Canoe Area is kept pristine by restrictions more severe than in most other places: no motorboats on most of the lakes, no snowmobiles. Not even airplanes may fly below a certain altitude. The silence sounds good to the people who launch canoes to refresh themselves from our asphalt and neon world. It sounds good to everybody except the people who live here. What most people in Ely want to hear in this wilderness is jackhammers mining the metals and chain saws cutting down the trees —at least some of the metals and some of the trees—to help the local economy.

They held yet another environmental hearing up here last week. Nearly all the speakers said they have had enough of silence in Minnesota's north woods. People here have had enough, as one speaker said, of environmental hearings and more than enough of legislators in other parts of the state telling them how to run their lives.

This is an often repeated story in America right now. The shrinking wilderness provokes attempts to save it, to save at least a few square miles of it. But that means keeping out the miners and loggers and developers—even the local people who have spent their lives in the area and have come to think of it as theirs.

The only people who really want to drain the Everglades and turn it into farmland are some of those who live nearby and would like to profit from those farms. The only people who want to cut down the

California redwoods are the people who live there, who make a living turning redwood trees into shingles and picnic tables.

Local people, who have more reason than outsiders to love the natural beauty they live with, find beauty hard to cash in on, so they are always the first to favor its destruction. You always hurt the one you love.

VERDI, NEVADA. The Evergreen Truck Stop sells a little diesel fuel, but when I was there this morning, it appeared to be doing a bigger business in toys and jewelry. The telegraph office was busy, and the slot machines were whirring and clanging. Truck stops are becoming cities.

At least one is officially a city—Little America, Wyoming. It's on the map. Little America has sixty-five gas pumps, and when I stopped there in the middle of the night it had at least that many trucks, their drivers gassing up, having a snooze, buying a stereo tape, getting a shoeshine. It's a long way from San Francisco to New York, and an icy road through the mountains. Little America is a place for a trucker to take a deep breath before terrifying the tourists in the mountain passes of Interstate 80.

The little Ma and Pa truck stop with the homemade pie is gone. In its place has risen a multimillion-dollar palace. There's one in Pennsylvania that cost $4.5 million to build and does more than that much business in one year. It has a barbershop and a honeymoon suite. Jarrell's Truck Plaza on I-95 in Virginia pumped 14 million gallons of gas last year. The Big Tex Truck Stop outside Dallas serves 50 gallons of coffee a day and isn't even in the big leagues. Jarrell's buys its coffee by the ton.

Truck stops today have pool rooms and color television lounges, scales, showers, telegraph offices, swimming pools, and doctors on call. Also on call are pretty young women in Corvettes who park on the fringes of the lots making their arrangements by CB radio. "Just blink your lights when you come in, honey," one of them said to an arriving truck driver one night in Oklahoma. Every truck in the lot started blinking its lights. Truck-stop owners try to discourage prostitution, but they have learned that if you operate a pleasure palace, you cannot exclude illicit pleasures.

These Interstate Alcazars now number about two thousand. The National Association of Truck Stop Operators says that ten years from now there will be four thousand. If the trend keeps up, all interstate highways from coast to coast will be bordered, eventually, by one long truck stop offering massages and manicures, games of chance, handball courts, and twenty-four-hour gourmet restaurants to the truck drivers. And, of course, diesel fuel to any who feel they really must leave.

RED LODGE, MONTANA. Alice Mitchell of Aberdeen, Washington, says she is planning a vacation trip with her family. She says in her letter to me, "You have been on the road for as long as I can remember. So tell me, what are America's most beautiful highways?"

All right, Mrs. Mitchell, here goes.

The most beautiful road in America is U.S. 212, which leaves Red Lodge, climbs to Beartooth Pass at eleven thousand feet, and drops down into the northeast entrance of Yellowstone Park. Don't try it in winter, Mrs. Mitchell; U.S. 212 spends the winter under many feet of snow. When the road opens, usually in May, the folks in Cooke City set up a booth to give the first day's intrepid motorists free drinks on the way through. It's that kind of highway. There will still be snow up there in August, but it's America's most beautiful road.

Second is California Route 1 along the coast from Morro Bay to Monterey. That's the road William Randolph Hearst built his castle on. (He'd have built his castle on the Red Lodge–Cooke City highway if he'd known about it.)

Third is the Going to the Sun Highway across Glacier Park. Fourth is U.S. 550 in Colorado, from Montrose to Durango. Fifth is Hawaii Route 56 from Lihue to Haena on the island of Kauai, but where the island really gets pretty is where the road ends and you have to start walking.

The sixth most beautiful road in America is the Blue Ridge Parkway in the spring. Seventh is Vermont Route 100 in the fall. Eighth is a road chosen for what's on it, U.S. 61 through Vicksburg and Natchez to New Orleans. Ninth is chosen for what's not on it, North Carolina Route 12 down the Outer Banks from Nags Head to Hatteras and by ferry to Ocracoke Island. Those are America's most beautiful roads. Anybody want to argue? Oh, and then, Mrs. Alice Mitchell of Aberdeen, Washington, there's Route 101 around the Olympic Peninsula. But you know that. That's the road you live on.

NILES, ILLINOIS. The leaning tower of Pisa stands—leans—on Touhy Avenue. I've never known why, but there it is. It enriches the drive down Touhy Avenue. A little north, in Milwaukee, there's a Chinese pagoda gas station. In Florida there's a seashell shop that you enter by walking into the yawning concrete jaws of a giant alligator. These are relics.

I like America's screwball architecture, but it's being replaced everywhere by humorless glass and steel. This is a loss. The interstate highways have done in all those hamburger stands that were shaped like hamburgers; remember them? A historian named Peter H. Smith shares my view. After a few years of commercial archaeology, Mr. Smith says we ought to establish a museum of the American highway to preserve the alligator-jawed gift shops before they're all replaced by carbon-copy modular gas stations. You hardly ever see even a World War Two fighter plane sitting atop the roof of a diner anymore. There used to be squadrons of them.

And the Brown Derby in Hollywood—tell me, is it still there in the shape of a big brown derby? And is that papier-mâché dinosaur still a gas station in Nebraska? And are they still selling Indian souvenirs out of a two-story concrete tepee in Wyoming? They were last time I passed that way, but America's gaudiest buildings are going fast.

Once the roadside was richer. In the twenties and thirties, if you ran an ice cream stand that *wasn't* shaped like an Eskimo pie, you couldn't keep up with the competition. Lighthouses, windmills, and giant cowboys beckoned at every mile to the motorist of a slower time. There were hot dog palaces in the shape of hot dogs and car washes in the shape of whales and drive-in movie palaces by the architect of the Taj Mahal. I mean, double arches are nice, but remember those two-story doughnuts on the top of doughnut shops? They have crumbled and we are poorer.

NOME, ALASKA. I was out in the Bering Strait with a boatload of playful Eskimos when one of them looked at the landmarks on the horizon, paddled our walrus-skin boat a few feet, and asked me, "What day is it?" "Friday," I said. "Nope," he said. "It was Friday a minute ago, but now it's tomorrow, Saturday. How do you like it?" I said it felt funny. Then he paddled us back into Friday again.

Even before I watched an Eskimo play footsy with the International Date Line, I was a little leery of time zones. I don't really understand them, and I don't care for them much. If you're in Wendover, Utah, at three o'clock in the afternoon and walk across the street, you have an hour to wait until it's three o'clock again. The time zone runs right through town. People in Wendover are very specific when making appointments.

If you fly from Lexington, Kentucky, to Evansville, Indiana, on Eastern Air Lines Flight 378, you take off at 9:30 in the morning and you get in at 9:05. *You* may be able to get used to the idea of arriving before you depart, but I never have been able to.

Theoretically, time zones divide the country from east to west, but in fact, they divide the country from north to south in countless crazy places. I left Goodland, Kansas, at eight o'clock one morning to drive thirty-nine miles due north to Bird City, where I was supposed to be at nine o'clock. But when I got there, it was nearly ten. The time zone in that part of Kansas is a booby trap, running cunningly east and west. I had lost a whole hour, and so far nobody's given it back to me. If you drive south from Canada, you can cross the time zone fourteen times before you get to Amarillo without moving west as much as fifty miles. If people in Kansas, Nebraska, and the Dakotas wear a slightly baffled look, it's because nobody knows what time it is.

Of all the states, Alaska is in the worst trouble. Here they have Pacific Standard Time, Alaska Standard, Bering Standard, and a cutie called Yukon Standard. You can lose an hour anytime you turn around, and if you go out with a boatload of Eskimos, you run the risk of losing a whole day.

SALT LAKE CITY, UTAH. I'm on the western slope of the weak coffee belt this weekend, and mornings are an ordeal. You can see through Salt Lake City coffee to the bottom of the cup. Drinking Salt Lake City coffee is like drinking hot water with a faint and distant memory of caffeine. There is an atavistic link somewhere, but coffee it is not. Salt Lake City coffee is to coffee what kissing your sister is to sex.

Coffee is coffee in New England. Coffee is fine in New York and Pennsylvania. Southerners make exceptional coffee, sometimes; it's a ritual in Charleston and a religion in New Orleans. But when you head west, something happens, something insidious, stealthy, treacherous. Independence, Missouri, is about where you begin to notice it. By the time you've crossed the river into Kansas, there can be no mistake. You have two or three cups of coffee for breakfast in Topeka and notice that your heart isn't started yet. By the time you get to Denver, the stuff doesn't smell or taste like coffee. At Grand Junction it doesn't *look* like coffee. Cross the Wasatch Mountains into Salt Lake, and there's nothing to do but buy yourself a coffeepot and brew your own. There's nothing resembling coffee to be had in a café until you reach the Sierras and drop down toward Sacramento.

Probably there's a historical basis for this. The pioneers, pushing off across the Missouri River, quickly ran out of coffee and had to start reusing the same grounds. Their children grew up liking it that way. The Mormon pioneers who peopled Salt Lake City rejected coffee as a brew of the devil, and their descendants figure, apparently, that if they aren't going to drink coffee around here, neither is anybody else.

Californians, of course, got fresh supplies by schooner around the

Horn, so California coffee remained drinkable. But from Kansas City to Reno, when the waitress says in the morning, "Would you like a cup of coffee?" I smile and nod and watch glumly what she pours into the cup and say to myself, "Oh, would I ever!"

Salt Lake City coffee is America's weakest. Some say Brookings, South Dakota, but they are people who haven't been to Salt Lake City.

LENHARTSVILLE, PENNSYLVANIA. By now, you must have seen a hex sign even if you aren't Pennsylvania Dutch—the starbursts and rosettes and whirligigs and flowers that the old Dutchmen put on their barns to keep the witches out. Drive through Lenhartsville or Fleetwood or Hamburg or Virginville and you can see them yet, fading now, some of them, but still up there near the roofline of the old barns, doing their job.

There used to be a hex sign painter here in Lenhartsville named Professor Johnny Ott. A farmer up on the Delaware River asked him for a rain sign during the drought of fifty-five, and pretty soon after the farmer put it up, the rain started falling, the river started rising, and the flood washed away the barn, the hex sign, and the houses of all the neighbors. "You damn fool," Johnny Ott told the farmer, "you put it up but you forgot to take it down."

Professor Ott's successor is a bearded Dutchman named Johnny Claypoole. Johnny fancies up his hex signs with distelfinks and tulips and once in a while a shamrock. He says the shamrock is historically justified, that some Irishmen in Washington's army painted the first one on a hex sign during the Revolution and chanted, "Hurrah for the Irish, they're not much. But they're a damn sight better than the Pennsylvania Dutch." Tourists buy the shamrocks from Johnny, but I've never seen one on a barn. Barn signs are serious business—the five-pointed star for good health, the eight-pointed star for goodwill, tulips for faith, oak leaves for strength, and most common of all, rosettes for luck. Luck is what every farmer needs most, as every farmer knows, and the rosette is easy to draw. You can do it with a pencil and a string if you haven't got a compass. It is the rosette you see everywhere, weathering gently into the 150-year-old siding on the massive red barns of the Pennsylvania Dutch.

I stopped in Jacob Zook's store down at Lancaster and bought a little rosette hex sign for the bus I travel around in. A big truck just missed me on the way out his driveway. Missed me, I say. He might have missed me if I hadn't had the hex sign. *Might* have, I say.

SAN ANGELO, TEXAS. Me, I can take chili or leave it alone, which makes it a good weekend to stay out of Texas. The International Chili Society is having its annual bourbon guzzle, beer bust, and chili cookoff on the banks of Dirty Woman Creek in the ghost town of Terlingua. Terlingua is occupied 364 days of the year by horned toads and tarantulas, and one day by columnist Frank X. Tolbert and assorted others who share little but the conceit that each of them makes the world's finest and hottest bowl of red. This contest is one with such other Texas competitions as who has the meanest rattlesnake and who has the ugliest armadillo. Texans will bet on anything.

The Terlingua chili-head competition is a mostly male affair. Texas women, who ordinarily have more sense, have started the Hell Hath No Fury Like a Woman's Chili Society, and I believe they are having their Third First Annual Amelia Jenks Bloomer Women's World Championship Chili Cookoff in the metropolis of Luckenbach. So, the length and breadth of Texas, there is almost no escaping the vile vapors of simmering chili.

Some people really like chili, apparently, but nobody can agree how the stuff should be made. C. V. Wood, twice winner at Terlingua, uses flank steak, pork chops, chicken, and green chilis. My friend Hughes Rudd of CBS News, who imported five hundred pounds of chili powder into Russia as a condition of accepting employment as Moscow correspondent, favors coarse-ground beef. Isadore Bleckman, the cameraman I must live with on the road, insists upon one-inch cubes of stew beef and puts garlic in his chili, an Illinois affectation. An Indian of my acquaintance, Mr. Fulton Batisse, who eats chili for breakfast when he can, uses buffalo meat and plays an Indian drum while it's cooking. I ask you.

As for me, I am going to look around San Angelo tonight to see if I can't make a meal of Scottish smoked salmon and a glass of Pouilly-Fuissé, leaning as I do toward Colorado Red Fenwick's opinion that chili isn't Texan at all. Chili was invented, Red says, by a Wyoming sheepherder to keep the feet of his sheep dogs warm on cold nights. He sent some to a Texas friend who ate it by mistake, which Texans have been doing ever since.

PHILADELPHIA. This old city is full of joiners. There's a club on every corner. Nowhere does the outsider feel as far outside as in Philadelphia.

The clubs announce themselves with plaques of bronze: "Acorn Club Members Only." The Cosmopolitan Club, the Downtown Club, the Ukrainian League, the Irish Center, the Italian-American Beneficial Society, the Polish-American Citizen and Harmonia Club. The Angling Club, the Archery Club, the Lawn Bowling, Boxing, Rifle, Chess, Bridge, Rowing, Golf, and Tennis clubs. The Driving Club. The Merion Cricket Club. The Mystic Knights of the Sea, the Royal Pythons, the Rabbits, the Vagabonds, the Leprechauns. The Hog Island New Year's Association.

Some clubs sound democratic, like the Forty-eighth Ward Democratic Club. But who wants to join a democratic club? The whole idea of proper clubs is to keep people out. I think my favorite is the one over in Devon. It is called the Chosen Few.

I've never been much of a joiner myself. The day I got my honorable discharge, I promised myself I wouldn't join anything else. I confess, however, that if I hung around Philadelphia very long, I might find myself staring wistfully at one of those bronze plaques and wishing I were in, not out. But how do you get to be a Rabbit or a Leprechaun if you are not one already? Only Rabbits and Leprechauns know.

I think I am eligible for the Bald-Headed Men of America. Motto: "If you don't have it, flaunt it." Telly Savalas comes to club meetings to throw darts at the Tom Snyder dartboard. "The Lord is just, the Lord is fair," goes the club song. "He gave some brains, the others hair."

I might find a home in the Millard Fillmore Society, established to honor the memory of our thirteenth president, who did nothing in the White House, which, the society says, was just enough. I like the dues structure, thirteen dollars with thirteen years to pay.

And I admire the Flat Earth Society, as we all must admire people who stick to their beliefs. The Flat Earthers examine evidence and do not accept theory. So far they've never found enough evidence to persuade them that the earth isn't flatter than a pancake.

Cousins to the Flat Earthers are the members of the Man Will Never Fly Society, which meets annually at Kitty Hawk to give an award to the person who did the most during the previous year to discourage the idea that flight is a logical thing. I approve of the society's description of itself as a "tongue-in-cheek, bottle-in-hand" organization, and of its motto: "Birds Fly. Men Drink."

I am sure you know of the National Association of Professional Bureaucrats. That's the organization that raced the U.S. Mail on horseback from Philadelphia to Washington awhile back and won. The Bureaucrats publish the Inaction Line and claim as their motto: "When in doubt, mumble."

But I think the Philadelphia club where I would best fit in is the famous one at Broad and Locust, the Procrastinators Club. Its members share the belief that anything worth doing is worth postponing. Their biggest success was their protest against the War of 1812; they staged the protest in 1966. The Procrastinators have a Christmas party coming up in June. I'd like to attend, but I'll probably put it off.

NEBRASKA CITY, NEBRASKA. Long thoughts from little acorns grow: Whatever happened to Arbor Day?

The answer, in Nebraska City, is that Arbor Day is the next big holiday after Easter. Here there will be a parade and much planting of trees. Nebraska City *cares* about Arbor Day.

The reason is that this was J. Sterling Morton's home. He came out here in 1854 from the lush green abundance of New York State and found something missing—trees. He started pushing trees on Nebraska. Even after he became Grover Cleveland's secretary of agriculture, he worried more about trees than today's agriculture secretaries worry about the Russian corn crop. J. Sterling Morton badgered state after state into declaring an Arbor Day like Nebraska's. In my North Carolina youth I was given a dogwood sapling by an indifferent schoolteacher and told to plant it, or else.

The trouble is, nobody agrees when Arbor Day is. It's next week in Nebraska, but it was last week in New Jersey and week before last in Missouri. It's a legal holiday in Rhode Island, and they let the kids out of school to plant trees in Colorado, Nevada, and New Mexico—though most of them just goof off, of course—but in Alaska, where planting trees is hopeless, they just ignore the whole thing.

Arbor Day is a big mess, to tell you the truth. Five counties of Arizona say Arbor Day is the Friday following the first day of April. The rest of Arizona says it's the Friday following the first day of February. Louisiana says Arbor Day is the second Friday in January—that is, if the state school board remembers to proclaim it at all. Texas

has copped out. In Texas, Arbor Day is the same day as Washington's Birthday.

Nebraska is dogged about Arbor Day, following the precept of J. Sterling Morton, who said, "If you seek my epitaph, look around." The trouble is, if you look around closely, you will see America's trees being turned into pulpwood and shipped to Japan. We have taken to thinking of trees as fuel, furniture, paper, and shingles; what J. Sterling Morton had in mind was beauty and shade. Check what happens to beauty and shade when they need to widen a highway. If you seek his epitaph, look around.

DEEP GAP, NORTH CAROLINA. There was a big crop of walnuts and acorns this fall and an abundance of woolly worms, and as everybody around here knows, that means a hard winter. But down the dirt roads and back in the hollows, you don't hear anybody complaining about the energy crisis. In these mountains, from the time Daniel Boone wandered up from the Yadkin River through the Cumberland Gap, people have been self-sufficient as to energy and they still are.

These thoughts came to mind when I stopped by to see my friend Willard Watson. He doesn't have a car to burn up gasoline, doesn't have a phone, and if it came to it, he could light his whole house for a month on seventeen cents' worth of kerosene. Willard was busy this fall with his ax and his feathers and wedges, so his woods are clean of trees felled by last winter's storms and his woodpile is twelve feet high, all beech and oak and maple, enough to keep him and his wife, Ora, cozy until May. Ora hasn't been feeling well—she thinks her blood pressure is up—but if the energy crisis got so bad nobody could take her to the doctor, she would probably get by on sweetgum bark or Indian poke tea, the way her mother did when the blood pressure was bothering *her*. Anyway, she has not felt so bad that she has neglected making a dozen beautiful mountain quilts in the last eight months. Willard and Ora have sixteen country hams hanging in the smokehouse, seven gallons of blackberry wine in the cellar, and all the corn and okra and tomatoes of the warm summer put up in neat jars in the pantry. The old cow still gives milk, the old hens still give eggs, and when one hen stops doing so, she still makes a fine Sunday dinner with dumplings, and the old wood stove still turns out better buttermilk biscuits than most of the rest of us have ever tasted in our lives. Water comes down into the house by gravity from a pure spring in the mountain above, a spring so prolific that Willard and Ora just let the water run all the time to ensure against the pipe freezing.

I spent part of my own youth in such a house away at the other end of the state in the flat coastal plain, and there, and here, such houses still are found. To city folk, which most of us are these days, the energy crisis means the threat of losing our jobs or not having enough gas to drive in to our jobs from the suburbs. Here in Deep Gap, where most people work only for themselves and have nowhere to go and do not depend upon machines, the only energy crisis conceivable would be not having enough children to milk the cows or slop the hogs or help plow the mule come spring.

We have called such people backward. Who is backward now?

CHICAGO. The fellow in the hotel room next to mine is taking a shower. I know because I can hear the water running. Last night he had a fight with his wife on the telephone. In hotel rooms these days, you almost always find out a lot about the guy in the room next to you because of the way they make hotel room walls these days—thin. The guy next door is usually better entertainment than whatever is on television.

People ask me, "What do you do with your spare time out there on the road?" And the answer is, I listen to the guy in the next room take showers. And dream, sometimes, of the perfect hotel room. It would be quiet. It could be made dark for sleeping because the curtains would fit the windows. It would have an adjustable shower head. It would have a rubber stopper in the sink, because mechanical arrangements for keeping the water in the sink hardly ever work and rubber stoppers do. Its color television set would show Walter Cronkite the way he really looks, instead of purple. It would have a radio. Aw, what the heck, since we're dreaming, it would have an FM radio. It would have an electric alarm clock, so it wouldn't

matter if the telephone operator got involved in her gothic novel and forgot my wake-up call. Its telephone would be at a desk, instead of beside the bed.

In the perfect hotel room, the laundry bags would accommodate more than one shirt and one pair of socks before tearing. The maids would not congregate outside my door at 6:30 A.M. to laugh and chat, and they would not knock at 7:00 to see if the "Do Not Disturb" sign is on there by accident. There would not be a picture of Montmartre on the wall of the ideal hotel room or, indeed, a picture of any other place in France. Once, in a string of Holiday Inns across four states in the Middle West, I got the same picture of Montmartre five nights in a row.

In the room of my dreams, I could turn down the heat, and—I hesitate even to mention it—I could actually open the window. Probably that's going too far.

Well, the guy in the next room has finished his shower. Now I can hear him putting on his socks.

CASTINE, MAINE. The National Weather Service says Castine, on Penobscot Bay, can expect sixty days of fog every year. This old town got seven of those days behind her last week and this. It was Thursday before the wind shifted around offshore and blew the fog back down into the islands off the coast and opened a view of the harbor for the first time in a week. This is hard on the lobstermen and the scallop draggers feeling their way among the rocks to try to make a living, and hard on the passengers bundled up on the decks of the tourist schooners, straining for a glimpse of the sparkling coast that is mentioned in the brochures.

The horn at Owl's Head light never got a moment's rest for a week, but the fog that is so hard on mariners and tourists is easy on the blueberries. They are ripening in the woods, and every roadside café in Maine has a hand-lettered "Blueberry Muffins" sign in its front window these foggy mornings. Blueberries need moisture. Without the fog, there would be no blueberries. Without the fog, there would be no ferns or mosses that make the misty coastal woods of Maine the most enchanting on earth to walk in, spongy and fragrant. The fragrance is given by spruce and cedar and fir, ghostly giants. There is an anchorage around a point of land where the fog was so thick that the fir trunks and limbs on land could hardly be distinguished from the fir masts and crosstrees at sea. Conifers love this weather. Without the fog, there would be no firs.

The firs, the rocks, the lichens, the berries, the birches, and the tamaracks, the seals and gulls that make this meeting of land and water the loveliest I know, all like the fog. When it finally lifted on Thursday, the tourists unzipped their windbreakers and came out blinking into the sun, dazzled by the green shore and blue water. "Isn't it beautiful?" they said.

But it wouldn't be, without the fog.

NORTH PLATTE, NEBRASKA. A letter came from Mrs. Conrad Green of Nantucket, Massachusetts. "In 1944," she wrote, "my husband and I were crossing the U.S. in a troop train. He was going out on a navy carrier from San Francisco as damage control officer. We boarded the train in Miami, Florida, and were three days with cold box lunches, not even coffee for breakfast, when we came to a stop and the conductor told us to get off. We went into the train shed, which was a big canteen with hot coffee and all kinds of hot food. When we tried to pay, they said no, it is our war work. . . .

"Imagine," Mrs. Green wrote, "two or three trains a day in each direction filled with three hundred or so servicemen and their dependents. . . . I shall always remember the people of North Platte, Nebraska, with tremendous gratitude."

Sounded fascinating, so I stopped by North Platte and found Rose Loncar, an original organizer of the North Platte Canteen.

"Yes," she said, "we served up to ten thousand a day, and never one serviceman or woman paid for a thing.

"It wasn't just the city of North Platte, either," she said. "It was people for two hundred miles around who brought hot food, home cooked, and we never ran out of it. It was almost like the Bible, feeding so many with a few loaves of bread."

The original idea, Mrs. Loncar said, was coffee and cookies at the station, and from there it just grew. Sandwiches started coming in, and homemade pies, and then fried pheasants in season and sides of barbecued beef and birthday cakes. No U.S.O. funds or government money, she said, just people from the farms and ranches and towns who couldn't stand the idea of so many young American men and women passing by on the train on the way to war with nobody to tell them a warm good-bye.

"I guess," Mrs. Loncar said, "that we hoped maybe somebody, somewhere, would treat the boys who had left our town the same way."

The railroad has knocked the depot down, and Rose Loncar said a lot of memories went with it. She said she thought the North Platte Canteen had been forgotten, after all these years.

Well, I didn't think it ought to be.

WEST HARTFORD, CONNECTICUT. I watched students of West Hartford's Bridlepath School compete in that vanishing standby of American education, the spelling bee. The spelling bee was held in Noah Webster's kitchen. That was a good place for it, because if it hadn't been for Noah Webster, we might never have had spelling bees or even much spelling. Before this Yankee schoolmaster came along, Americans spelled poorly or not at all; George Washington, to cite one atrocious example, spelled pretty much as he pleased. After Noah Webster, Americans spelled the way Noah told them to.

The kids in the spelling bee came from all kinds of backgrounds and from all over the country. That they speak the same language —that a kid from Maine can meet a kid from Oregon and understand him right from the start—that is Noah Webster's gift to us. His little Blue-Backed Speller sold nearly 100 million copies in his lifetime. It wore out printing presses. It was read by nearly every American who could read.

And then, working for twenty-five years, alone and by hand, Noah Webster produced his dictionary—seventy thousand words, including a lot of American words that had never been in a dictionary before: *applesauce, bullfrog, chowder, hickory, skunk*. It was the most valuable piece of scholarship any American ever did.

Noah Webster, from this old house in West Hartford, created American style and American manners. It is not too much to say that he created American education. He was the first teacher of American history, the first influential American newspaper editor.

"What rubbed Mr. Webster's fur the wrong way," West Hart-

130

ford historian Nelson Burr told me, "was that even after the Revolution, most of America's books and most of America's ideas still came from England. He wanted to put a stop to that. He wanted to create Americanism—not in the sense of jingoistic patriotism, but in the sense of a new literature, a new language."

In the Italy of Noah Webster's day, there were so many dialects that many Italians couldn't talk to one another. The same thing, to a lesser degree, was true in Great Britain. America's common language, with more or less agreed-upon rules for spelling and punctuation, was the work of Noah Webster. He wanted us to be one nation, a new nation, and he showed us how.

KITTY HAWK, NORTH CAROLINA. I come from North Carolina, and it is true that if you come from North Carolina and mention that fact to anybody anywhere else, you will get this reply:

"Oh, yes, I have an aunt who lives in Charleston."

The only solution for this is for South Carolina to change its name, but South Carolinians being conceitful, that isn't likely. Dakotans have the same problem, of course. George McGovern may have helped make the distinction between the Dakotas by rising to national prominence from one of them—but quick, now, which one? Millions of Americans know that George McGovern is from Fargo or somewhere out there. This is also a problem for West Virginians, "West, by God, Virginians," as they say up there in the democratic hills, to distinguish themselves from the aristocratic lowlanders to the east. And you would be surprised at the volume of mail addressed every year to Richmond, West Virginia. New Hampshire, New Jersey, and New York avoided this curse by taking the names of provinces from which they are separated by a broad ocean—but only a step separates us progressive Tar Heels from them barefooted South Carolinians, and the rest of the country doesn't seem to know the difference.

People cannot get it through their heads that *South* Dakota is the one that has Mount Rushmore, and *South* Carolina is the one that has Strom Thurmond. North Dakota is the Flickertail State, while South Dakota is the Coyote State, or, let's see, is it the other way around? There's probably no use worrying about it, people's geographic ignorance being what it is.

West Virginia has actually considered changing its name and

may yet one of these days. Jim Comstock, the estimable editor of the *West Virginia Hillbilly,* says they were discussing the issue in class at West Virginia University one day, the professor arguing for a change. "*West* in the name of the state hurts us," he said. A football player in the back of the room objected: "It hasn't hurt West Consin, has it?"

DALLAS, TEXAS. Last night in the restaurant, I heard the fellow at the next table say he was taking a day off to go sculling. His companions just nodded and moved on to the next subject, which bothered me because I wanted some questions answered. Sculling? I thought people went sculling only on the Thames. Where do you go sculling in Dallas, Texas? Why do you go sculling at all? And—since I am a product of the Puritan work ethic—when *you* go sculling, buddy, who's minding the store?

With a will, I managed to restrain myself from asking all these questions, but I have been brooding about them ever since. We live in a time when men shut down the lathe early to get in a little hang gliding before supper, and women ignore their children to go jade prospecting—a time, indeed, when the owner of the stuffiest financial journal in the country, *Forbes* magazine, doffs his cravat and bowler, turns his back on the moguls and millionaires who depend upon him, and toots off on a hot-air balloon trip across the country.

I have been *working* my way across the country for more than a decade now, and every year has brought a quantum leap in time off for everybody else. Lately even lonely country roads are aswarm with joggers, including many old enough to know better. Whole clubs and regiments of Americans routinely devote their days off to iceboating or spearfishing. More than once have I slammed on my brakes to avoid turning a skateboarder into a pancake. Every youth in America is riding a bicycle from New York to California. Dowsing is hotter than ever, also kung fu and psychocybernetics. Gnomics, sky walking, snowshoeing, flea training, bridge diving, mud bathing,

freight train hopping, dressage, and water polo are catching on. Herb growing has never been more popular. Massage, wine making, and dervish dancing are coming into their own. So are falconry and sleep learning. Backgammon is back, which means Mah-Jongg is surely coming back. There are birdhouse-building clubs all over the country. Beekeeping, beachcombing, and beagling are big and getting better.

They are sculling in Dallas! So if the gross national product is declining, do not ask complicated questions to know the reason why. Just ask how many knapsacks, telescopes, tape recorders, and dune buggies the Japanese worked to make this year so that Americans could play. I guess the gross national product is not the most important thing in the world, but if it's important to you, ask Malcolm Forbes what he was doing up in that hot-air balloon.

BOONVILLE, CALIFORNIA. Boonville is not one of your auto-motive repair centers. There are a couple of gas stations that can give you a lube job, and five miles up the road at Philo, there's Brownie, who has a wrecker, but if you suffer a major breakdown in Boon-ville, you're going to be in Boonville for a while. I can assure you of that, because this is where the gallant old van that transports our CBS News crew around the country has broken down. This time.

Last time was fifty miles down a dirt road in the middle of Wyoming. Two flat tires and two bent rims, which is one tire and one rim too many. That led to our having to spend the night at the home of the nearest rancher, whose wife fixed delicious elk steaks for us. The two of them sat up late with us, talking, one of the best evenings of good whiskey and good talk I can remember, and then put us to bed between clean sheets under beautiful handmade quilts.

The old bus's engine blew up one time in Stuttgart, Arkansas. That happened to be right in the middle of the best duck-hunting country in the U.S.A., right in the middle of duck-hunting season, with a two-day wait for a new engine to be trucked in from across the state.

In fact, now that I think of it, some of the richest experiences in our years of wandering across the country have come when we were forced, by a wrenching sound in the transmission or the crack of a broken axle, to come to a sudden *halt* in our wandering. We never *wanted* to break down, of course, but looking back on it, I can't re-member ever being sorry we did. Forced us to get out, look around, meet a few people, and hear a few stories.

It was a burned-out wheel bearing this time, and so the old bus is sitting right now in Jack June's driveway, supported at the right rear by five sturdy white oak logs, pending a new brake drum, which must come from far away. Jack June turns out to be a wonderful man, forester, naturalist, artist, fly fisherman, and raconteur, and Janese June is likewise a woman of spirit, with much to say and an engaging way of saying it.

On balance, I recommend a transmission failure or burned-out wheel bearing from time to time. It messes up your schedule and forces you to get to know the country.

GREENVILLE, MISSISSIPPI. A copy of the *Boston Globe* has made its way down here with an editorial of unintended wit. This Boston writer says mud is a thing of the past. America has conquered mud, he says. The highways are paved, he says; so are the driveways; so are the shopping center parking lots; nobody remembers the spring season known as mud time.

Well, galoshes may not any longer be necessary on Beacon Hill, but here in the Mississippi Delta, hip boots will not suffice. It is muddy. Lord, it is muddy. People around here are beginning to doubt the teaching of the Old Testament, because this very spring it has rained for forty days and forty nights and not even an ark could get through the soybean fields, it is so muddy.

Here is this Brahmin up there walking around on Boston asphalt and remarking prettily on the conquest of mud, and the whole midsection of America is sinking in it. That editorial writer should have been with me last month on Willis Grumbein's mule farm in Dodge City, Kansas. *That* would have mussed up his wing tips. Missouri's even worse. A man from Blue Eye stepped out of his bass boat onto what he thought was the shore of the Table Rock Lake in April and was up to his chest in five seconds. His partner got a line under his armpits just in time and hauled him out with the Evinrude. By July that shore will be baked out, but in April it's Missouri mud than which there is no thicker. I travel around in a sort of bus, and I parked it in Eddie Lovett's yard in Banks, Arkansas, last week. Next time I looked, it was going down by the stern. It took three jacks, eleven

two-by-fours, and an hour and a half to get it back to the high ground.

It has been a muddy spring. "So thoroughly has America been covered over," this editorial writer from Boston laments, "that the kids don't know what it's like to make a mud pie."

I passed some kids in the Delta the other day helping their folks clean a foot of Mississippi mud out of their house, where the river left it, and wish now I had thought to show them the editorial. What kids these days really don't know is what it's like to have a good laugh.

GATLINBURG, TENNESSEE. This is the time of year when country people used to take a little molasses for their health. Every table had a jar of molasses that was never removed. It stayed there with the salt and pepper, a necessity. You had a little with your biscuits for breakfast and with your cornbread for dessert, and in the month of March to stay well.

There used to be a song: "I like molasses, good old country sorghum, I eat it in the spring and in the fall. And when it trickles down my chin, I just lick it off again, and that's the way I like it best of all."

Nobody has a strong enough stomach to eat molasses anymore, and that may be why everybody is so sickly. These days molasses is looked upon not as a product but as a by-product. It is what is left over after the sugaring process. Kansas feed lots give it to the cattle. Maybe you have noticed that cows hardly ever catch cold.

Well, I like molasses, good old country sorghum. You may correct me if I am wrong about this, but I believe the good stuff is appreciated nowadays only in certain remote hollows of east Tennessee. They still keep ancient sorghum mills in operation there, with a mule patiently plodding around in circles to grind the cane, a bucket covered by cheesecloth to filter the syrup and keep the flies out, and skillful old men to heat the syrup over wood fires in big evaporators until it has bubbled just enough to be thick and black and sulfurous. Then they take it off the fire and pour it in fruit jars in sufficient amounts to last out the year. This is rich and splendid fare, far too good for any Kansas steer, and widely coveted among those with taste, and memory.

The story is told of a Tennessee mountaineer telling a friend, "Those people over in Pigeon Forge sure do love sorghum. I had a fool yesterday offer me his mule for this here gallon of my molasses. His mule was worth a hundred dollars and this molasses could only fetch a dollar and a half."

"Did you make the trade, then?"

"Well, of course not, this here's all the molasses I've got."

CONVICT LAKE, CALIFORNIA. I had a good supper here last night. I mention this because in an age of fast food, a slow supper is hard to come by.

People ask me how I spend my time on the road. I spend more of it than I would like CBS to know about looking for a good restaurant. If you have your supper in public three hundred nights of every year, sooner or later your definition of a good restaurant becomes any place that does its own cooking. It might be a fancy restaurant in New York, or it might be a café in Arkansas with a $1.99 blue-plate special and a cook out back who knows how to cook. Both these places are scarcing up, as they say in Arkansas. What you find instead are places with names that have something to do with kings or foxes or coaches or horses. They have decorators, but they do not have cooks. They make frequent use of the word *gourmet*. As soon as you see the word *gourmet,* you can be sure you're going to get a frozen TV dinner that has been warmed up in the microwave oven.

Much food is not even food. They are making gravy out of chemicals now. They call it old-style country gravy. They are making bacon out of soybeans. They are mixing seaweed and gelatin and calling it pineapple. I had a hamburger the other day with grill marks on it. A good sign, I thought. No, a bad sign. The grill marks were painted on.

Cream used to come in pitchers. These days it comes in little plastic trapezoids that are inventions of the devil. They cannot be opened without squirting cream all over your shirt. Anyway, it isn't cream. It isn't anything that ever saw the inside of a cow. If you get

any of it into your coffee instead of onto your shirt, what it tastes like is water, hydrogenated palm kernel oil, sodium caseinate, sugar, dipotassium phosphate, propylene glycol monostearate, polysorbate 60, stearolyle-lactilate, salt, artificial flavor, and color. That's what it tastes like because that's what it is. The advantage over cream is that it costs less and doesn't spoil as fast. Note that this is an advantage to the coffee shop, not to the coffee drinker. A further advantage is that waitresses, whose lives used to be boring, are now steadily amused as one customer after another squirts himself in the chest and utters hilarious and innovative oaths.

Restaurant owners say it is all right to make food out of chemicals because it is nutritionally and calorically equivalent to real food. I am out here on the road eating equivalence all the time instead of supper, and I can tell you it is no fun.

Convenience foods are for the convenience of those serving them. The best example is the tomato. The tomato is a wonderful thing, but most Americans have never tasted one. Recent tests show that our cars cannot take a five-mile-an-hour impact without sustaining great damage, but the newest supermarket tomatoes can be dropped to the floor at fifteen miles per hour without being damaged.

I liked the suggestion of the *Los Angeles Times* that we ought to start driving tomatoes.

NEW CASTLE, DELAWARE. During the first half of the seventeenth century, when the nations of Europe were squabbling over who owned the New World, the Dutch and the Swedes founded competing villages ten miles apart on the Delaware River. Not long afterward, the English took over both places and gave them new names, New Castle and Wilmington.

For a century and a half the two villages grew apace, but gradually Wilmington gained all the advantages. It was a little closer to Philadelphia, so when new textile mills opened, they opened in Wilmington, not in New Castle. There was plenty of water power from rivers and creeks at Wilmington, so when young Irénée DuPont chose a place for his gunpowder mill, it was Wilmington he chose, not New Castle. Wilmington became a town and then a city—a rather important city, much the largest in Delaware. And New Castle, bypassed by the highways and waterways that made Wilmington prosperous? New Castle slumbered, ten miles south on the Delaware River. No two villages with such similar pasts could have gone such separate ways. And today no two places could be more different.

Wilmington, with its expressways and parking lots and all its other concrete ribbons and badges, is a tired old veteran of the industrial wars and wears a vacant stare. Block after city block where people used to live and shop is broken and empty.

New Castle never had to make way for progress and therefore never had any reason to tear down its seventeenth- and eighteenth-century houses. So they are still here, standing in tasteful rows under ancient elms around the original town green. New Castle is still an

agreeable place to live. The pretty buildings of its quiet past make a serene setting for the lives of 4,800 people. New Castle may be America's loveliest town, but it is not an important town at all. Progress passed it by.

Poor New Castle.

Lucky Wilmington.

ST. CROIX VALLEY, WISCONSIN. Here it is possible to be grateful to a glacier. When the last ice age ended and that massive mantle of ice retreated to the north, it left a gift behind—the landscape of Wisconsin. The runoff of millions of tons of ice, thousands of feet thick, carved out the valley of the St. Croix, arguably our prettiest river. The glacier gouged out Lake Superior, our loveliest and greatest lake. The churning, grinding ice left behind thousands of other rivers and lakes and hills and valleys and a glacial moraine where maple and oak and ash and aspen could grow, and beneath their branches, beaver and otter and raccoon and mink, and partridge and sharp-tailed grouse. This land covered by ice must have been a formless sight to see. But there was nobody here to see it, apparently. Nature used ice to prepare the land for us.

If there had been no glacier, there would be no trout in the Sunrise River, no happy summertime innertubing on the Apple, no wood ducks nesting in the old trees on the banks of the St. Croix. There would be no wild-rice harvest to look forward to in the bright cold mornings of fall. There would be no Wisconsin Rapids, no Wisconsin Dells, no Green Bay, and therefore, hard as it may be to accept, no Green Bay Packers. There would be no rich green fields for Wisconsin's herds of spotted dairy cattle, no dairies, no cheese. And, since beer comes in part from the rushing glacial streams, no beer.

The glacier did its work well. And scientists studying those days of Pleistocene miracles have chosen a good name for the last ice age. They call it by the name of the place it found as a waterless plain and altered into magnificence. The last ice age is known the world over as Wisconsin.

BALTIMORE, MARYLAND. I was waiting for breakfast in a coffee shop the other morning and reading the paper. The paper had sixty-six pages. The waitress brought a paper place mat and a paper napkin and took my order, and I paged through the paper.

The headline said, "House Panel Studies a Bill Allowing Clear-Cutting in U.S. Forests."

I put the paper napkin in my lap, spread the paper out on the paper place mat, and read on: "The House Agriculture Committee," it said, "is looking over legislation that would once again open national

forests to the clear-cutting of trees by private companies under government permits."

The waitress brought the coffee. I opened a paper sugar envelope and tore open a little paper cup of cream and went on reading the paper: "The Senate voted without dissent yesterday to allow clear-cutting," the paper said. "Critics have said clear-cutting in the national forests can lead to erosion and destruction of wildlife habitats. Forest Service and industry spokesmen said a flat ban on clear-cutting would bring paralysis to the lumber industry." And to the paper industry, I thought. Clear-cutting a forest is one way to get a lot of paper, and we sure seem to need a lot of paper.

The waitress brought the toast. I looked for the butter. It came on a little paper tray with a covering of paper. I opened a paper package of marmalade and read on: "Senator Jennings Randolph, Democrat of West Virginia, urged his colleagues to take a more restrictive view and permit clear-cutting only under specific guidelines for certain types of forest. But neither he nor anyone else voted against the bill, which was sent to the House on a 90 to 0 vote."

The eggs came, with little paper packages of salt and pepper. I finished breakfast, put the paper under my arm, and left the table with its used and useless paper napkin, paper place mat, paper salt and pepper packages, paper butter and marmalade wrappings, paper sugar envelope, and paper cream holder, and I walked out into the morning wondering how our national forests can ever survive our breakfasts.

ST. MARTINVILLE, LOUISIANA. The settlement of this country, in the national memory, was accomplished by the English. We sometimes forget the Spanish who were living the good life in St. Augustine when Philadelphia was still a muddy village. We overlook the Pennsylvania Germans and the California Chinese and the Minnesota Swedes—and the Louisiana French.

So stop beside the bayou in St. Martinville, where the hamburger stands sell *boudin, oreilles de cochon,* and *sauce piquante,* where the shoe store owner and the barber and the sheriff's deputy have names like Olivier, Dupré, and LeBlanc, and French lullabies are sung to children at night.

This is a quiet village with moss-hung oaks and broad streets, but no town in America has a more vivid history. It started as a fort, a military post built to protect the French indigo planters from the Indians. St. Martinville was utterly unknown to the genteel Virginians and the Massachusetts settlers chafing under George III, but it was a pleasant and prosperous town just the same.

Then came the Acadians, exiled from Canada because they refused to give up their Catholic faith. They came by ship and by incredible overland journey to swell St. Martinville's French population. They don't teach Longfellow's poems in school any longer, so we can't expect the young among us to know the story of Evangeline. But here in St. Martinville you learn that it was very nearly a true story that the poet told. In fact, Evangeline's name was Emmeline Labiche. Her Gabriel was named Louis Arceneaux. The live-oak tree where Evangeline and Gabriel had their brief reunion still spreads

its branches on the banks of the Bayou Teche. The day I visited it, the only other tourists were a middle-aged couple from Ohio, visibly touched, and their teen-aged daughter, visibly bored.

I walked across the street to the graveyard behind the Catholic church where a graceful statue of a seated Norman girl marks a tomb on which are inscribed the words "Emmeline Labiche. Evangeline."

I felt sad. Sad for Evangeline. Sad for the kids who don't read Longfellow anymore.

It was the French Revolution that brought St. Martinville its most unlikely immigrants—barons and counts and marquises and their noble ladies, all fleeing the guillotine. They imported a French opera company and gave great balls. They established nothing less than a miniature of Marie Antoinette's court in the Louisiana swamps. St. Martinville became known throughout the French-speaking world as Le Petit Paris.

English-speaking America has never known much about any of this. When Jefferson bought Louisiana in 1803, he made sure that the first code of laws forbade the cutting off of ears. The Americans thought this elegant French parish was occupied by savages! They had never heard of St. Martinville. So narrowly do we understand our national past that most of us still haven't.

LAKE HAVASU CITY, ARIZONA. I passed through here a few years ago and found old Arizonans amused by the notion that Robert P. McCulloch, the fellow who makes chain saws and drills for oil, had finally flipped his lid. He had bought the London Bridge, and he was going to ship it over from the River Thames, stone by stone, and put it up in the Arizona desert. Old Arizonans are conservative folk, you know, and if there was ever a more chuckle-headed scheme than that, they hadn't heard about it. But, of course, there is no stopping big dreamers, and pretty soon the stones started piling up in the sand in Lake Havasu City, McCulloch's dream town beside the dammed-up waters of the Colorado River. The stones had code numbers, painted on when they took the bridge apart so that Robert McCulloch would know how to put it together again. The old Arizonans said he'd never do it.

Well—he did it. I am standing here looking at it, and it's the London Bridge all right, and it looks rather grand. There are banners flying from the thing and cars traveling across it and tourists strolling under it, shops and pubs surrounding it, and an occasional old Arizonan wandering by, paying it no attention, as if the London Bridge in the desert were the most natural sight on earth.

The town around it has grown from a barren little outpost in the sagebrush into an inviting small city, and with the London Bridge as its centerpiece, the city is now visited by no fewer than a million people a year. People just have to come see the London Bridge. Robert McCulloch knew all along they'd have to.

So the old Arizonans aren't chuckling anymore. Anyway, the bridge was a bargain. Sure, McCulloch had to pay two and a half million dollars to buy it and another five million or so to ship it over and put it up again, but look at it this way: anything over a hundred years old is classified as an antique by the U.S. Customs. That makes the London Bridge the country's biggest antique, and Robert P. McCulloch didn't have to pay a penny in duty.

KANSAS CITY. Kansas City stands at the eastern edge of the wheat belt, at the western edge of the corn belt, and at the northern limit of the white belt. This is not a racial remark. I am talking about the white *belt,* which men in Kansas City have taken to wearing with red pants. White belts with red pants started in Texas and Louisiana, curved east through Alabama and Georgia, and then west through Tennessee and Missouri. This is the red pants fertile crescent, and it has cut down my contacts in these places, for I will never have anything to do with a man in red pants.

White belts and red pants usually lead on to white shoes. The streets of Kansas City are all a-strut with drip-dry Dacron-polyester peacocks in red pants with white shoes. They all feel natty. Male nattiness is puzzling and alarming.

Kansas City males should have paid closer attention to the estimable, departed Bill Vaughan of the *Kansas City Star,* who always held that American civilization started to decline when men ceased being rumpled. All the great men of American history were rumpled. Lincoln springs to mind. Edison. Clarence Darrow. Irvin S. Cobb and John Nance Garner and Wendell Willkie and Eugene Victor Debs. There were rumpled giants in those days. Things have been going downhill ever since pants got creases. Can you imagine John L. Lewis in red pants and white shoes?

Bill Vaughan wrote one time, "As I look back over traveled roads, I am struck by the fact that the men I trusted the most, the ones I voted for, hired to sue my neighbor for shooting my dog, or invited to plunk my anatomy for diagnostic purposes, were invariably

rumpled." Bill Vaughan wanted to bring back the seersucker suit or the white linen suit, which, when worn for as long as an hour, made a man look like a congressman who had just franked himself home in his own laundry box.

Most men in red pants, I have noticed, are old and fat. I am becoming old and fat myself, but before you see me in red pants, I will see you in hell. My favorite suit, of conservative three-button cut, is made of what Abercrombie and Fitch used to call safari cloth. Ten minutes out of the cleaners, it looks like it has been on a safari. I treasure it.

Beware the tidy dresser. Neatness marks a man whose emphasis is on all the wrong things. The political season will soon be upon us. I am looking at the candidates' clothes, not their voting records, and hoping for a wrinkled Lincoln.

NEW YORK CITY. Abraham Lincoln, Mark Twain, Alexander Graham Bell. I went up to the Hall of Fame this week to look into their faces.

John Adams, Susan B. Anthony, Henry Wadsworth Longfellow. Their bronze busts stand amid Corinthian columns under a majestic portico. The Hall of Fame for Great Americans was established in 1900 and was intended to last for the ages.

Audubon, Poe, Edison, Thoreau. All are enshrined in this marble colonnade on a height above the city.

But fame is fleeting, and marble crumbles. The city below the height is New York, a city going to seed. It cannot pay to keep up many worthwhile things nowadays, and one of the things it cannot pay to keep up is the Hall of Fame for Great Americans. The staff has been fired, the information booth closed. The Hall of Fame looks abandoned, like much of the neighborhood it is in. Leave the place to the weather and the chewing gum wrappers.

Ralph Waldo Emerson, Booker T. Washington, James Abbott McNeill Whistler, Thomas Finley Breeze Morse, Thomas Jonathan Jackson, known as Stonewall. The vandals, who do not recognize these names, may be expected soon to obliterate them by writing their own names in spray paint on the timeless columns.

A Hall of Fame is for heroes, and heroes are out of fashion. Oh, the baseball Hall of Fame is still alive, and the football Hall of Fame. There is, I believe, a Hall of Fame for accountants. These are commercial enterprises. There is money to be made from them, and they are doing all right.

But Oliver Wendell Holmes? Who might he have been? Well, he is one of the ninety-seven abandoned bronze busts in the Hall of Fame for Great Americans. A writer, in his day. One thing he wrote was this:

Ah, pensive scholar, what is fame?
    A fitful tongue of leaping flame,
A giddy whirlwind's fickle gust
    That lifts a pinch of mortal dust.
A few swift years, and who can show
    What dust was Bill and which was Joe?

POINT LOBOS, CALIFORNIA. This place belongs to the rocks and waves and otters and seals and birds. Man comes here as a stranger. You park well back from the coast and approach Point Lobos on foot, past a grove of fantastic gnarled and twisted Monterey cypresses, through the sea grasses and windblown chaparral. I have made this walk many times—Point Lobos is a pilgrimage—and every time I have felt small and out of place, a stranger in a perilous and majestic meeting place of land and sea.

I have seen a storm off Hatteras, and I have known a summer's day in Southwest Harbor, Maine, and I have watched the waves break on the rocks at Cap d'Antibes. Point Lobos is like none of these other beautiful places; Point Lobos's beauty is wilder and more dangerous.

Off there where an arch of the rocky headland collapsed hundreds of years ago, a great rock stands. It is home to the brown pelicans. At its base, in a bed of kelp, sea otters lie on their backs dining on sea urchins. There is a harbor seal. There is a *giant,* a sea lion. And there is a behemoth. A gray whale spouting a salute to Point Lobos as it passes.

Each wave that breaks boils into fantastic eddies of blue and white and sea green as it curves into the recesses of the coast and wears down the rocks another fraction of a millimeter. How changed Point Lobos must be from the headland men first looked upon! This place is an experience in space, and in time, too. It's not very large, a thousand acres of space for time to work upon. Just to the north, men have made the picture-book village of Carmel, and to the south

the coast is also built upon and tamed. This place, these rocks and islands and fog-washed pinnacles and crashing waves, this place has resisted man and taming. Come here, if you can, someday. But don't expect to feel at home.

NEWPORT, RHODE ISLAND. I went to religious services this week in a Jewish synagogue, a Baptist church, and a Catholic cathedral, and I'd have dropped by to see the Buddhists, too, except that nobody answered the door at the Zen temple. This outbreak of ecumenical churchgoing was just my way of revisiting Rhode Island, which is the first place in this country where people could be Jews or Baptists or Catholics or Buddhists, even, without somebody else coming after them with a gun.

Religious liberty is so old in America that we've forgotten where it started. Well, it started here, when Roger Williams got himself kicked out of Massachusetts for nitpicking the Puritan sermons. That was in 1636, a while ago. Roger Williams wanted to start a place where anybody could believe anything. His idea was to protect the church—any church—from the state, a little different from Jefferson's idea 150 years later that the state had to be protected from the church. But it led to the same thing, freedom of conscience, a long time before the rest of the country got around to agreeing that was a good idea.

Within a few years of its founding, naturally, Rhode Island was full of nonconformists, strange types, Quakers and Baptists and Antinomians and Anglicans and Jews. All the people who didn't fit in anywhere else settled down here and argued with one another. It must have been chaotic, as different from Puritan, monolithic Massachusetts as brawling, raucous democracy always is from neat, totalitarian order.

That's why I went to church this week. To visit the country's oldest synagogue, the one here in Newport to which George Wash-

ington wrote, "The government of the United States gives to bigotry no sanction, to persecution no assistance." And the Baptist church in Providence, which Roger Williams founded in 1638. (Lots of cities have a First Baptist Church. Providence has the *first* Baptist Church.) And the old Catholic cathedral, which is still the center of arguments in Rhode Island over abortion and state aid to parochial schools. That's all right. For 340 years around here, religious arguments have come with the territory.

TUSKEGEE, ALABAMA. "Booker T. Washington will do."

That is what the village of Tuskegee replied to the president of Hampton Institute in Virginia. Tuskegee had asked for a Hampton graduate to start a school for black boys and girls in Alabama. The Hampton president replied that the only suitable candidate was named Booker T. Washington, born a slave, educated by persistence, and only twenty-four years old. This man didn't sound very promising, but this small town knew that what it had to offer him wasn't very promising either. So the reply was sent: "Booker T. Washington will do."

He arrived in 1881. He had no money, no students, and no prospects. He went out into the countryside to meet the people. He met a black man of sixty and asked him about his background. "Born in Virginia," the man said, "and sold into Alabama." "How many were sold?" Booker T. Washington asked. "There were five of us," the man said. "Brother and me and three mules."

In a time and a place where men thought of themselves as animals, Booker T. Washington started a school. The first building was a dilapidated shanty of a black church in such a state of disrepair that during rainstorms one student held an umbrella over the head of the teacher while he tried to teach the others. On weekends Booker T. Washington drove about in a wagon drawn by a mule to round up new students. "There will be a new building," he said, "made of brick. We are going to build it ourselves. This will be a college course in bricklaying."

He said later, "Without regard to pay, and with little thought

of it, I taught anyone who wanted to learn anything I could teach him."

To this place came former slaves and their children, many of whom did not know much more than how to chop a row of cotton. They made intense students, and in time Booker T. Washington gave them great teachers, among them the gentle agricultural revolutionary George Washington Carver.

Booker T. Washington sent into our national life thousands of educated black men and women who took up the struggle for a freedom more real than anything the Emancipation Proclamation could guarantee. The visitor on a pilgrimage to Tuskegee finds that struggle still going on in farm fields and classrooms and laboratories. The founder of this university knew that knowledge is freedom.

We are looking for heroes of this country's stuttering effort to provide justice and dignity for all our citizens. Booker T. Washington will do.

SPRINGFIELD, ILLINOIS. In Springfield you can ride in a Lincoln cab. You can play golf at Lincoln Greens, check out a book from the Lincoln Library, buy insurance from Lincoln Life or a drink from the Lincoln Tavern or a carburetor from Lincoln Auto Parts.

Honest Abe would be amused by all this and know that no disrespect is meant by those who commercialize his name. On the contrary, it is entirely understandable, if you own a barbershop in Springfield, Illinois, to wish to name it the Abe Lincoln Barbershop. After all, people in Postville, up the road, named the whole town for Lincoln —Lincoln, Illinois. And every license plate in the state bears the legend "Land of Lincoln."

Well, I don't know if Chicago is the Land of Lincoln, but Springfield certainly is. His house still stands at Eighth and Jackson, and townspeople who have treasured a rocking chair or a walking cane that once belonged to the Lincolns slowly have been returning them to the house. Today it's much as Lincoln left it when he made that speech at the depot in 1861:

"My friends, no one, not in my situation, can appreciate my feeling of sadness at this parting. To this place, and to the kindness of these people, I owe everything. Here I have lived a quarter of a century, and have passed from a young man to an old man. Here my children have been born, and one is buried. I now leave, not knowing when, or whether ever, I shall return."

So even Lincoln acknowledged that this is the Land of Lincoln. After you visit his house, you can stop by the depot where he made that speech and the law office where he and Billy Herndon shared those small fees, never refusing to do a favor, always ready to defend poor people in court for no fee at all.

You can visit New Salem, a few miles away, where he lived as a young man, the village that first sent him to the state legislature.

And you can go out to Oak Ridge Cemetery, where he is buried. His tomb, and that of Mrs. Lincoln and three of their sons, is a 117-foot spire with four heroic groups of bronze soldiers struggling at the base. It is garish and overwrought. But when it was built, it was an effort of Springfield's people to show that they returned his pride in them and love for them.

The Abe Lincoln Barbershop is something like that, too.

GRAND ISLAND, NEBRASKA. The homesteaders out here on the Great Plains haven't been so wrought up over anything since the days when William Jennings Bryan went from hamlet to hamlet thundering against the gold standard. What has Nebraskans outraged this time is art—ten sculptures that have been placed at rest areas on Interstate 80 as a Nebraska Bicentennial project. Even before the sculptures came into existence, the project directors made the mistake of putting pictures in the newspapers of how they were going to look, and you could hear the bellow of outrage from Omaha to Scottsbluff. The actual placement of the sculptures hasn't moderated Nebraska scorn one bit. "Monstrosities, created by mountebanks!" says one letter to the editor. "Junkyard rejects!" says another. "Grotesque structures," writes a barnyard critic from Ogallala, "which despoil the horizons."

Such other matters as sex and taxes have been known to rile Americans up, but as a general rule we do reserve our truly deep, fun-

damental indignation for modern sculpture. Much is being made here of the fact that none of the ten sculptors is from Nebraska. Seven are from the East Coast, that suspect and subversive distant region; two are from the iniquitous West Coast; and one is from the community of Northfield, Minnesota, a lesion on the map of the Middle West.

The sculpture selected for the interstate rest stop several miles from Grand Island is one called *Erma's Desire* by an artist from Boston. You'd think several miles might be far enough to render the community safe from the thing, but the board of supervisors agreed unanimously that it does not want *Erma's Desire* anywhere in Hall County. It voted to investigate the matter and hold public hearings.

Nobody knows yet how this is all going to turn out. I remember similar controversies over that Picasso in Chicago and the St. Louis arch. In those cases, public opinion since has turned toward coexistence, if not affection.

But I wouldn't count on tolerance breaking out in Nebraska just yet. These are the people who beat back the grasshopper and the drought, and they surely have it in them to win out over art.

KENT, OHIO. This morning a snowflake fell on my sleeve. This is hardly the kind of occurrence of which profound coast-to-coast radio network analysis is made. A snowflake falling on your sleeve is the opposite of an earth-shaking event, and of course it's earth-shaking events we're always talking about on the radio. But let me tell you about that snowflake.

The Ohio snow shower was ending, and the sun was coming out, and the flakes had grown large, the way they do sometimes just before the snow stops, so I really got a good look at it. It was luminous and perfect, a patch of crystalline lace, but brighter than lace, dancing with brittle reflections.

Now—being conscious of the suspicions of a suspicious age, I have to assure you at this point that I am not a user of hallucinogenic drugs or anything. That snowflake was beautiful.

This is something every child knows, of course, and I suddenly realized, standing there in the cold, that while in the last thirty years I have more than once been snowed on, have stuck automobiles in snow, have sat impatiently on airplanes delayed by snow, I have never once, since I was about eight, looked at a snowflake. Well, I recommend it. Children, who are delighted by the snow, are right. They look at snowflakes one at a time, which the rest of us have forgotten how to do.

While admiring that snowflake this morning, I remembered holding a baby trout in my hand for an instant last summer before slipping him back into a mountain stream. I remembered a fern I once looked at—really looked at—on the floor of a redwood forest. The trouble is that after childhood such insights into the small perfections of nature are mostly lost among the large imperfections of our own creation. We love playing God, but our washing machines don't work, and every trout and fern and snowflake does.

I raised my arm to get a closer look at the snowflake and brought it too close to my face, and it melted. If you breathe on beauty, it is gone. But it comes again for those who aren't always looking somewhere else.

NEW YORK CITY. I have arranged to meet her in the lobby of her hotel at seven. It's been a long time. I didn't think anything like this could make me nervous anymore, but there it is, undeniably, that small knot in the stomach that I remember from all those years ago.

I'll be going straight from the office to meet her, so I dressed for dinner this morning, gray suit, white shirt. I tried two or three ties before I found the one I thought would look best. I stopped for a haircut. I had my shoes shined. All this is silly, at my age, I know that. It's not as if the world would come to an end if things didn't go right tonight, after all. She is only a woman, after all. But when I had my egg salad sandwich at my desk this noon, I found myself being absurdly cautious that no egg salad dribbled out on my tie, the one I had chosen after two or three tries.

I sent flowers to her room; I hope she won't think that is excessive. White carnations. I remember she used to like carnations. I thought of champagne, but that would be going too far; I don't want to be too obvious about this. I suppose I don't want her to know how much this means to me.

I made reservations for dinner; oh, I did that ten days ago after a lot of thought. I was going to take her to "21," that was my first idea, but then I thought she might find that too showy. She has always had quiet tastes. And besides, to be perfectly honest, they might not remember me at "21." They might give us an obscure table. So I made the reservation at a little place on East Forty-eighth Street instead. We'll have fondue and white wine. She grew to like fondue, I remember, that summer in Europe. So it should go well—a romantic dinner in a small restaurant, a walk up Fifth Avenue afterwards—we have a lot to talk about, after all. And tomorrow maybe the Cézanne exhibition at the Museum of Modern Art. I don't know why I'm so nervous, waiting for this evening. Maybe every man feels this way who has a daughter coming down from college for a weekend in the city.

WASHINGTON, D.C. I saw James Earl Carter sworn in as "Jimmy." Heaven only knows why a man with a strong biblical name like James wants to be a president named Jimmy. I'm certain that if he were named Charles, he wouldn't fool around that way.

Charles is not so bad, but Charlie is a terrible burden to bear. There have been kings named Charles: Charles the Bold, Charles the Great, as well as, I believe, Charles the Bald and Charles the Fat. England's next king will be named Charles—Charles the Broke, if things keep going as they are over there. You can't be a king named Charlie.

You can be a president named Jimmy, obviously, though Jimmy Madison, Jimmy Monroe, and Jimmy K. Polk might have counseled against it. But Charlie is simply impossible. I have friends who call me Charlie, but not very good friends. Good old Charlie. Good old Charlie, in a new book by Peter Chew about the difficulties of being a middle-aged man, is a kind of lustful incompetent. Mr. Charlie. Mr. Charlie is, in black lingo, the bumbling white overlord who is laughed at behind his back. Good-time Charlie—a drunk making a fool of himself.

It is no accident, I'm sure, that when the cartoonist who signs himself Charles Schulz wanted to invent a symbol of haplessness, to be picked on by the world, he named him Charlie Brown. Charles has a little dignity. Charlie, no matter how you look at him, is no better than a genial fool.

People with incorruptible names like Matthew are always calling people named Charles, Charlie. I wish my folks had named me Matthew. Matt is the worst that can be made of it, and Matt Dillon

is a square-jawed sheriff. Who can imagine Charlie Dillon? A square-jawed name like Matt would have been nice, as in Dillon, or a robust athletic name like Hank, as in Aaron, or a serene, intellectual name like Eric, as in Sevareid. If you are named Charles and take a trip to Minnesota or the Dakotas, do you know what they call you? They don't even call you Charlie. They call you Chuck.

MARQUETTE, MICHIGAN. We say that the Irish who came to America brought a gift of good talk and poetry, the Germans brought thrift and energy, the Italians a love for music. I don't know about all that, but after a few days in the Upper Peninsula of Michigan, I am certain of the contribution of the Finns: sisu.

I heard a man say of his neighbor that he had sisu. When I asked what sisu is, the man dug up an essay for me to read. It was written by Dr. John I. Kolehmainen of Heidelburg University, and it gave me a scholarly understanding of sisu. It's hard to translate, but it means something like guts—courage, doggedness, persistence, the ability to accept reversal and go on.

The Finns who settled the ragged wasteland of the Upper Peninsula needed all the sisu they could get. This was a logged-over, burned-over land. The Finns decided to farm it. It is pretty widely agreed that nobody else could have taken such a desert of stumps and stones and turned it into a land of neat furrows and tidy houses—nobody but the Finns. They did it with axes and plows and sisu. The men put in back-breaking days of stern hard work and self-denial. The women, they say, worked on an eight-hour schedule: eight hours in the morning, eight more in the afternoon, plowing and sowing, hoeing, digging ditches, cutting hay with their men.

"The Finn is singular," wrote a visitor who watched the first-generation Finns at work up here, "in that sooner or later he is conquered by an unreasoning, mad passion to own his own place. . . . He has to have something, if only a birch tree, a spruce, or a pine, a goat or a cow, around which he can fling his arms and exclaim, 'This

no one, not even the richest lord, can take away from me!'" Almost all the Finns of the Upper Peninsula came to own their own homesteads. It took sisu, and they had more of it than anybody else.

Drive through here now, notice the pretty houses and barns and meadows resting under the snow, and if you know a little local history, you cannot help admiring the Finnish sisu. And if you have been reading the morning papers, you can't help hoping that in times like these, some of it will rub off on the rest of us.

SAN FRANCISCO. Charlie Quinlan, a member of a camera crew I worked with, poured himself another beer and said, "It's nice to get back to Frisco." The bartender loomed above him. The bartender smiled. "Please," the bartender said, "don't call it Frisco."

Don't call it Frisco. Herb Caen, who plays Boswell to this city's Johnson in the *San Francisco Chronicle,* wrote a book one time with that title, *Don't Call It Frisco.* Ogden Nash wrote a poem about boiling in oil or frying in Crisco if you ever make the mistake of calling it Frisco. So Charlie Quinlan should have been forewarned. New York is the Big Apple, Dallas is Big D, Los Angeles is L.A., Philadelphia is Philly, Detroit is Motown, and Chicago is Chi. These are all affectionate nicknames, and all accepted by the residents. But none of these other cities is as serene as San Francisco, as beautiful, or as self-conscious. Don't call it Frisco.

Truck drivers call it Shakytown, with earthquakes in mind. It was mariners, I believe, who first called it Frisco. Charlie Quinlan's problem is that he is an old navy man. He first saw Frisco from the

deck of a destroyer during the long-ago unpleasantness with Japan. No sailor ever called Frisco anything but Frisco, and all sailors loved Frisco shore leave.

Jack Smith, musing on the subject of Frisco from a safe distance, wrote in the *Los Angeles Times* that he remembers a song, "Hello, Frisco, Hello," and an old movie, *Hell on Frisco Bay*. Frisco, Jack Smith says, was always a term of endearment. But songs are written in the Big Apple, and movies are made in Tinseltown, and neither of those cities is properly sensitive to the overweening pride of San Francisco or the fragile preferences of its citizens. Frisco sounds merely breezy to me, but it sounds vulgar to the delicate ears of Friscans.

So call it narcissism. But don't call it Frisco.

MACKINAC ISLAND, MICHIGAN. Your carriage picks you up at the ferry dock and clip-clops you back into time. No cars permitted on Mackinac Island, this dot of green in the blue of the Mackinac Straits. From your seat in the horse-drawn carriage, you look serenely down on the "fudgies," as the islanders call them. Fudgies are the tourists who make the ferry trip from Mackinaw City just to walk around for the day, buy a pound of fudge, and go back to the mainland. It must be awful to be a fudgie when you can be a guest at the Grand Hotel.

There it is up on the hill, and a grand hotel it is, the largest remaining of those rococo wooden landmarks that sprouted like daisies in the daisy days of the Gay Nineties. Cornelius Vanderbilt had much to do with the building of this one, and in the fullness of time, Chauncey Depew came here to dance the Portland Fancy with Mrs. Potter Palmer, and the Fields and the Armours and the Swifts came up from Chicago and Adolphus Busch from St. Louis. They even let politicians stay here, as long as they had names like Theodore Roosevelt, Grover Cleveland, William Howard Taft.

Most grand hotels died out in the twenties and thirties, but W. Stewart Woodfill, an impeccable dandy of a man, would not let the Grand Hotel die. He took it over in 1923, and he is here again this summer, strolling smartly down the flower-banked veranda, swinging his gold-headed cane, and nodding to his guests. Mr. Woodfill has spent so much time out here on the island that he doesn't know Holiday Inns have taken over the hotel business. At this one place—my carriage is approaching it now—afternoon tea is still served, and tipping

is not permitted. There are rolling chairs and lawn games. Elegant couples stroll in sunken gardens. The orchestra plays waltzes.

Now we are at the foot of the sweeping driveway. There is a large sign forbidding gentlemen without ties or ladies in slacks even to walk on the street in front of the hotel after six.

Here is the scarlet carpet of the *porte cochère*. The carriage slows and stops. To tell you the truth, I'm a little nervous, and I hope Mr. Woodfill doesn't notice me. I admire his style, but he'll know at a glance that I'm a fudgie trying to pass.

PROVIDENCE, RHODE ISLAND. A writer in a Texas magazine, *Accent West,* raises the question whether there *is* a place called Rhode Island. Says he's never met anybody from here nor anybody who knows anybody from here. Says he watches the Cronkite news and can't remember an explosion or mass murder or scandal here. Says he doubts there is a Rhode Island.

Well, I have news for this Texan. Here in Big P, as people in Rhode Island call Providence, the capital, Rhode Island is beyond doubt. Rhode Island is not too different from Texas. It is every bit as far across the state of Rhode Island as it is from Midland to Odessa, about twenty miles, and it takes about the same length of time to make the trip on horseback. The range animal of Rhode Island is the Rhode Island Red, a somewhat smaller animal than the Texas longhorn, but one that stampedes less readily, consumes less grass on the range, and is easier to rope at Rhode Island rodeos.

The Sam Houston of Rhode Island was named Roger Williams. The streets of Providence still bear the names given them by Williams —Benefit, Benevolent, Friendship, and Hope. Those are a little different from such Texas place names as Buckshot, Cut 'n' Shoot, and Rattlesnake Butte, but there is a town in Rhode Island called Nooseneck, where Texans might feel at home.

Further Rhode Island information for Texans:

The cowboy of Rhode Island is called a clam digger and rides a boat. The Galveston of Rhode Island is called Newport. The cowchip-throwing contest of Rhode Island is called the America's Cup

Yacht Race. The Lyndon Johnson of Rhode Island is called John O. Pastore. The Oklahoma of Rhode Island is called Massachusetts.

Rhode Island is a small state, but spunky. Texas Goliaths who make jokes about how small it is should watch out for little kids with slingshots.

APACHE, OKLAHOMA. This country has too many chiefs and not enough Indians. I speak as a Kiowa myself. I was standing in a corner at a Kiowa war dance, reporting the homecoming of a couple of U.S. army warriors, when suddenly the dance ended and I heard my name mentioned, followed by war whoops. Somebody put a blanket over my shoulders. A lean and angry-looking man said, "Dance."

"I can't dance," I said. Somebody thrust a fan into one of my hands and a rattle into the other.

"We are turning you into a Kiowa," the angry-looking man said. "Dance."

"I don't even do the foxtrot well," I said.

"Dance," he said.

I danced. At either side of me were other large and muscular Kiowas in warpaint, dancing like mad. I felt compelled to smile, but nobody else was smiling. The compulsion to smile left me.

At length, at great length, the drums stopped. An old man named Cecil Horse, son of Hunting Horse, a Custer scout, made a speech in English and pronounced my Indian name: Blue Eagle. More banging of drums and whooping. I stood as erect and eaglelike as I could and tried to get used to the idea of being Blue Eagle while old man Horse made the same speech in Kiowa. When he got to the name part, there was a murmur in the room. He called me over. "I said it wrong in English," he said, embarrassed. "You are Bluebird, not Blue Eagle." As he tried to tell me this, his elderly wife kept shouting into his bad ear, "It's too late! You've already pronounced it! It's too late!" "It's too late," old man Horse said to me, "but you are Bluebird, not Blue Eagle." I told him that suited me better anyway.

Then the drums started again, and the chanting, and I felt proud, like Crazy Horse after the Little Big Horn. I turned to Izzy Bleckman, the cameraman with whom I work, and said, "Gee, last week they made me a Kentucky Colonel, and this week they've made me a Kiowa Indian."

Izzy said, "You are working your way up to Jew."

CHICAGO. A guy in a bar was telling me about the magician in Seattle who predicted the New York power blackout.

"I heard about it," I said. "I don't believe it."

"You don't *believe* it?" he said. "It was a fact."

"It was a trick," I said.

"I can't believe you don't believe it," he said.

"Believe it," I said. "You want to know what else I don't believe?" I said. "I don't believe in the Loch Ness Monster. I don't believe in the Bermuda Triangle. I think the Abominable Snowman is an abominable publicity stunt to promote tourism in Nepal."

"What about Big Foot?" the guy asked.

"Big Foot is a big put-on," I said. "So are UFO's. They always turn out to be swamp gas or the Goodyear Blimp."

"Yeah?" the guy said. "What about the UFO that landed in Pascagoula, Mississippi, a few summers ago and gave those two fishermen a ride?"

"Look," I said, "if there are beings on another planet intelligent enough to send a spaceship to earth, they are also intelligent enough not to land in Pascagoula, Mississippi, in the summertime."

The argument was getting loud and people started staring.

"What's your birth sign?" somebody asked.

"Virgo," I said.

"Virgos are skeptical," he said.

I said, "I do not believe in astrology." Everybody looked appalled. Somebody asked, "You don't believe in the Age of Aquarius?"

"I believe in the Age of Enlightenment," I said, "and we need one in this bar."

People started murmuring incredulously and pointing fingers at me, and I decided to let them have it.

"I don't believe in alpha waves," I said. "I don't believe in gurus from India or ancient astronauts from Venus. I don't believe in the Lost Dutchman gold mine or the Lost City of Atlantis. I don't believe in biorhythms. I don't believe in psychoanalysis. I don't believe in Marxism or mermaids or playing Mozart to houseplants."

"Far out!" the first guy said. "What *do* you believe?"

I considered the question. "I believe," I said, "that the Cubs have a chance to win the pennant."

The guy groaned. "Oh, man," he said. "If you believe that, you'll believe anything."

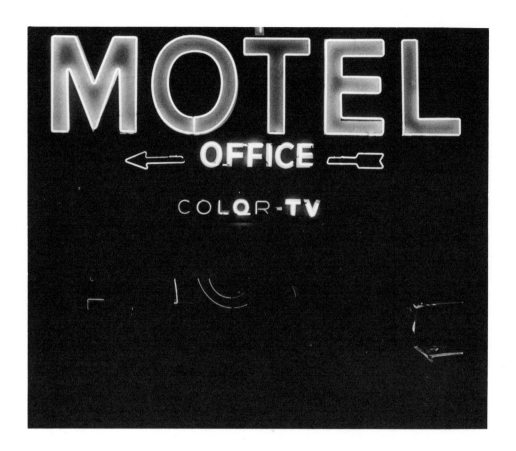

PORTLAND, OREGON. We all say our money isn't worth anything, but we mean it to be just a figure of speech. Well, this week I came across another of those places where money *isn't* worth anything.

At one of Portland's biggest motels, a grand-looking place that fronts on the Columbia River and advertises the warmth of its welcome to the weary traveler, it turns out they mean only the weary traveler with a credit card. When you check in, they ask you for your credit card. If you fork one over, the desk clerk smiles and the run of the place is yours. You may airily order meals and have champagne sent to your room and make telephone calls to Istanbul. If, on the other hand, you have only money, terrible things happen. The desk clerk does not smile. He demands your driver's license and turns it slowly over in his hand reflectively, examining it for erasures. He looks you over suspiciously for frayed cuffs or unshined shoes or intimations of fraud. He demands payment in advance. Only then does he permit you to sign in, pointedly insisting on noting your license plate number on the card. Then he turns his back, leaving you to carry your own bags guiltily to your room.

This is not treatment reserved only for suspicious-looking characters like me. If John D. Rockefeller were resurrected from the dead and walked into this motel's capacious lobby with a retinue of servants, two steamer trunks full of starched collars and afternoon coats, a diamond stickpin in his tie, and a pocket full of crisp thousand-dollar bills, this desk clerk, before permitting him to check in, would ask him for his credit card, and if old John D. laughed a deep-throated Rockefeller laugh, he would then demand that he pay in advance before noon on each day of his stay. That, I was informed, is the policy.

Well, John D. Rockefeller, of course, would just buy the motel on the spot and turn the flibbertigibbet desk clerk into the street. The rest of us can only fantasize, pay in advance, skulk away, promise ourselves never to patronize the joint again, and resume the narrowing search for an American hotel that still treats its patrons as guests, even if they come bearing cash instead of celluloid.

JONESBORO, TENNESSEE. What you need for breakfast, they say in east Tennessee, is a jug of good corn liquor, a thick beefsteak, and a hound dog. Then you feed the beefsteak to the hound dog.

That is one kind of east Tennessee breakfast, but it is not the kind I feel so lyrical about.

Eggs. But not eggs from a supermarket dairy case, eggs from a chicken. There is a subtle difference. What you do with these eggs is fry them in country ham grease in the same pan in which you have already fried your country ham. East Tennessee country ham is to Virginia ham what the sonnets of Shakespeare are to the works of Rod McKuen. It is salt-cured by hand, and hung in a smokehouse for time to work upon it, and sliced thin with a hacksaw, and fried. Country ham is a gift of God to east Tennessee.

After you have cooked your ham and cooked your eggs in the ham grease, you scrape the iron pan in which you have performed these miracles and add to the scrapings a spoonful of coffee. What you have there is red-eye gravy. No pen, unless it be filled with red-eye gravy, can describe the delights of red-eye gravy. It goes on your grits. These are not bland, instant grits out of a big round box. These are stone-ground, long-cooking, mouth-watering grits, fit grits for red-eye gravy.

Now you open your oven and take out your buttermilk biscuits. East Tennessee feels sorry for people who eat toast. Now you take your dish of sweet butter from the cool place in the pantry. Now you fill your cup with hot black coffee. Now you sit down with your country

ham and country eggs and grits and red-eye gravy and buttermilk biscuits and fresh butter and hot coffee and say thanks.

What I say thanks for is the one place in our country where they
still believe in, and practice, breakfast.

KALISPELL, MONTANA. Driving along the Kootenai River today, I came upon a scene that looked like the aftermath of World War Three. The forest had been cut down, right to the tops of the ridges. A formerly beautiful mountain had been stripped, and nothing was left but an infinity of stumps. It was a horrible sight, but what made it worse was a sign that was placed by the side of the road in front of this devastation. The sign said, "Good Forest Management for a Growing America." It went on to explain how good it was for the trees to cut them down.

This use of words to say the opposite of what is meant is bad, and it's getting worse. At many supermarket checkout counters, they now photograph you if you write a check, with a little built-in camera. At most motels they demand identification before permitting you to check in. Both these spreading customs are irritating enough, but what makes them infuriating are the signs that come with them. Both signs are written in large type, and both begin, "For Your Protection." Of course, these damnable practices are not for your protection at all; they are to keep you from writing a bum check or from stealing the TV set in your motel room. If the signs would just say that, it would help a little.

The worst sign of all is the one that comes with that hot-air hand dryer in the men's rooms of restaurants too cheap to provide towels. "For Your Convenience," the sign says. "Prevents Chapping." What those hand dryers really do is prevent the management from having to pay for towels, prevent you from getting to the meal you're so hungry for while you shift from one foot to the other waiting for your hands to dry, and (speaking for myself) prevent me from ever going back there if I have a choice. I know what's for my protection and what's for my convenience, and I also know what's a lot of hot air.

ROANOKE, VIRGINIA. The crocuses are up. I have seen the first daffodils, too, and a line of geese flying north.

But these are not the surest signs that the season is changing. The surest sign is that yesterday I saw a kid stretch a playground single into a double with a gaudy slide. The dust cloud that he raised was so stupendous that it obscured the whole basketball season, with its nasty little episodes of college players stomping one another while down, and the football season, with its endless excess of big-money bowl games. At last it is the baseball time again. Sweetness and sanity return, and the earth renews itself.

It has been a long winter. College football is to games what General Motors is to the neighborhood garage. Basketball might have been a good game when they played it with a peach basket; now they play it with big money. The L.S.U. basketball coach read a story in a newspaper about a minister in Florida who said he had seen a hairy creature about eight feet tall in the Florida swamps. The coach wrote to the preacher, "In case you see him again, I would appreciate it if you would have him call me collect as we would like to offer him a full basketball scholarship." I thought the spring would never come.

Poll takers and soothsayers, their eyes upon the box office, proclaim baseball to be a dying sport. They should travel the land in the spring and shift their gaze to the vacant lots. Nothing, nothing has changed. Nine-year-olds still take mighty practice swings holding the bat at the very end, for to choke up on the handle is to admit you are not yet a man. The ball is wrapped in black friction tape to keep it from unraveling. The catcher wears his cap backwards but takes the

pitch on the first bounce, because who has a mask or chest protector? The ten-year-old shortstop still talks it up to the eleven-year-old pitcher —"Make him hit it to us, baby!"—and prays to God that if he does hit it, it doesn't come too low and hard to handle. The fat, slow kid still plays right field.

Those who predict baseball's death never swung from the heels and, wonder of wonders, actually connected and sent the ball on a low arc over the infield and rounded first to see, wonder of wonders, the outfielders still chasing it. A triple! After all those swings that stung your hands and resulted in weak fouls and timid pop-ups, a legitimate, honest-to-goodness triple! The muscles of millions of American men still remember the precise feeling, the time it didn't sting. It was a miracle, which recurs every March. That is why baseball, the best game, will never die.

I watched the game end yesterday. The boy who owned the ball had to go home to supper. The players swaggered away into the twilight in dusty camaraderie, just the way we used to swagger. Suddenly I remembered my fifth-grade teammates' names, Tommy Watkins, Bill Savage, Darrell Kirkpatrick, Bobby Sparks. Where are you now, fellow swaggerers? The season is here, and I don't have anybody to play with.

CHAPEL HILL, NORTH CAROLINA. Losing has been much on my mind lately. My baseball team, the Yankees, has been losing in spring training. My basketball team, the University of North Carolina, lost the national college championship to Marquette. A television enterprise I am involved with has been losing in the ratings. I am losing my hair and my eyesight. I'm beginning to feel like a loser.

A loser is the worst thing you can be in America. Winning, as Vince Lombardi did or didn't say, isn't everything, it's the only thing. Defeat, as Coach George Allen did say, is like death. We are a country of winners, which is what made the Vietnam War so hard to take. A winner never quits, a quitter never wins. When the going gets tough, the tough get going. I remember all those maxims from the walls of dressing rooms and the offices of officials of the Nixon administration.

Well, I don't know. I guess I *am* a loser. North Carolina's defeat to Marquette was agonizing at the time, but I liked the way they lost, struggling down to the final buzzer, then shaking hands with the winners, standing up straight and applauding as the other guys got the trophy. And I liked the coach they lost to, Al McGuire. He isn't the coach who said, "Winning isn't everything, it's the only thing." He's the coach who said, "Winning only counts in war and surgery." That's un-American, that remark, but that doesn't make it any the less true.

Probably we need to offer a course in losing, since somebody loses every game. To teach the course, I nominate Ed Walsh, the superintendent of recreation in Westbury, Long Island, who wrote in the *New York Times* the other day, "There's no laughter in losing . . . and that's a pity, because when we lose laughter, we lose joy. Because the dread of losing dominates our sporting lives, we have bleached the fun out of colorful games."

Winning *isn't* the only thing, Coach Lombardi. Defeat is *not* like death, Coach Allen. I noticed the daffodils came up in my garden the morning after the Marquette game, even though North Carolina lost. Life goes on, even for us losers. I have a new maxim for the dressing room walls: Berton Brayley's sportsman's prayer, which says, "If I should lose, let me stand by the side of the road and cheer as the winners go by."

BILOXI, MISSISSIPPI. "Never!" That's what the rednecks and Ku Kluxers used to shout at the suggestion of human progress here, and their T-shirts were emblazoned, "Never!" That was about ten years ago. I stood for a while one day this week watching black and white kids playing together in a churchyard at recess from Bible school and listened for an echo of that shout and couldn't hear it. In the blink of an eye, historically speaking, the South has changed fundamentally and forever.

In the Delta the heavy rains have given the weeds a head start on the cotton, and the weeds will have to be chopped out by hand. Cotton chopping used to be mostly a segregated occupation, but now, in many fields, black and white work together, talking and joking. And all must receive the federal minimum wage now, which makes the old back-breaking work a little easier.

In one of the new commercial catfish ponds up near Hollandale, young black men and young white men worked together, up to their knees in the water, and at a filling station outside Jackson where one black man worked with a number of whites, it was he who took our gas money and gave change from the cash register. He was the manager. The white men in the place worked under him, not the other way around.

These changes may seem slight and trifling to you if you did not grow up in the South. To a native son returning, they are so strange and wonderful as to lift the heart.

Not that all changes in the South are heart-lifting. Progress is a sharp blade, double edged. There's a lighted sign on Peachtree Street in Atlanta that tells you the city's population: 1,466,721. Every minute

or so it blinks and the number changes: 1,466,722. There are times—
like the times when you're stuck in a sweltering traffic jam on Peachtree Street with nothing to look at but the blinking sign—when you
wish it were going backward, winding Atlanta down to the tree-shaded,
civilized city it used to be before progress set in. The South, which
has gained so much of justice, has lost a good deal of grace. Waitresses
who used to call you "honey" while serving you your grits now word-
lessly clunk down your hash browns and turn away without caring
that your coffee cup is empty. There are 1,466,721 other people to be
served, and there is no time for courtesy, let alone for small talk. When
asked to check the oil, gas station attendants in Alabama roll their
eyes to heaven in expert imitation of their Yankee cousins.

What is happening, of course, is that the South is becoming like all
the rest of the country. The band played "Dixie" in a restaurant in
Tallahassee the other night, an event that used to guarantee lunatic
hollering and cheering, and nobody in the place even looked up from
his glass of cold duck. All over Alabama and Mississippi the tarpaper
shacks are coming down and the Holiday Inns are going up. Public
health officials here used to worry about pellagra among the children
of the poor; now, according to a story in the Birmingham paper, they
are worrying about VD among the children of the prosperous. Atlanta's boring superhighways and new architecture of glass and aluminum
are indistinguishable from the superhighways and skyscrapers of, say,
Pittsburgh. They do not advertise Big Red chewing tobacco on color
TV in Pittsburgh, but that is the only difference between the two cities
that springs to mind.

But if this new sameness is the price the South has had to pay for

the new decency, it seems a small price. At breakfast in Gadsden, Alabama, I sat across the room from four beefy state patrolmen who were having a coffee break, their big revolvers sticking out into the aisles of the café. These were the policemen who seemed to take such pleasure in breaking the heads of black civil rights marchers and northern reporters just a few years ago, and anybody who was here in those days, as I was, would have taken a table a respectful distance from those officers, as I did. But I could hear what they were talking about: their golf games. One of them said he was having a lot of trouble with his approach shots.

"Never!" the white demonstrators used to shout, waving their ax handles. The black marchers sang a soft song back to them: "We shall overcome, someday." I wasn't sure then, but now I know that history in my native region belongs to the singers of that song.

At the big Panther Burn plantation not far from here, they're bulldozing the old shacks of the field workers and building modern houses and making it possible for the workers to buy the houses instead of renting them, as before. The candidate who won the Democratic primary for Congress from this district was a white civil rights worker in the sixties; the coalition that won for him included both former freedom riders and former Klansmen. The black mayor of Fayette was host of a big picnic this week. People born black in Mississippi came back from New York and Chicago and Los Angeles to attend. They called it a homecoming. There was something to come home to.

GREAT FALLS, MONTANA. The woman at the next table at supper the other night paid her bill, left a tip, laid her napkin on the table, dumped the whole bowl of sugar envelopes into her purse, and left.

Sugar, at this writing, is $2.25 for a five-pound bag. "Stolen waters are sweet, and bread eaten in secret is pleasant," saith Proverbs 9:17, and the restaurant owners saith people are calling for more rolls, bread, butter, and sesame seed crackers and just sweeping them off into their pockets and purses, so Proverbs must be true. The Bible also says, "Thou shalt not steal," but that was written before sugar went to $2.25 and bread to 60 cents a loaf.

This is getting to be a real problem, according to Larry Buckmaster, who is head of the Illinois Restaurant Association, and so some restaurants are fighting back, serving sugar one envelope at a time, doling out bread by the roll and crackers by the cracker. And, of course, there's a simple solution for the filchers of ketchup bottles—just leave the cap off. Rare is the ketchup thief who will risk sticking the bottle in his pocket uncapped.

Now, speaking for myself, I would never dream of stealing a ketchup bottle, with or without a top. But since I've been old enough to go to restaurants, I admit that I have routinely drunk my iced tea without the lemon. That is so when I have finished the iced tea, I can squeeze the lemon into the glass, add water and sugar, and experience the thrill of a free lemonade.

This is strictly small-time stuff, by today's standards. A motel manager in Grand Junction, Colorado, told me about a young couple driving a camper who checked in recently. Said they were on their honey-moon. Ordered dinner in their room. Stole the cream, the sugar, and the rolls. Stole the coffeepot. Stole the silverware. Stole the television set, the lamp, the chairs, the tables, the bed, the carpet, the mirrors, and the bathroom sink.

What made the motel manager mad was that he sent them a bottle of champagne and they never even thanked him.

TULE LAKE, CALIFORNIA. This is a sight to stop your heart. In this one place at this one time, two million water birds are flying in from the north in formations that stretch as far as the eye can see. They bank out of the sun, glide toward this lake, spread their wings, and splash gently down. The Klamath Basin on the Oregon-California border is the greatest waterfowl area in the world. Right now I am looking at more than 100,000 snow geese. I have to turn in my tracks to see all of them.

This place is the neck of an hourglass. Geese from the west turn inland and cross the Cascades to get here. Birds from the Northwest Territories change course at the Snake River in Idaho to join the convention. Other birds come from still farther east, across the prairie provinces, across the Great Salt Lake, to add their gabble to the Babel of the Klamath Basin in November.

What are they doing here? They might ask what *we* are doing here. The geese got here first. Long before there were any Russians in Siberia, the geese came south from Siberia. Long before there were any Canadians in the Northwest Territories or Alaskans in Alaska, the geese came south from there. And long, long before there were any of us in California or Oregon, the snow geese from Siberia and Alaska and Canada, winging south across what are now international boundaries, stopped here at this lake to feed and rest. The Russians think of the Siberian geese as theirs, and the Canadians consider the geese of the Yukon theirs, and we say, "Look! Our geese are coming in from

Alaska!" But the geese carry no passports. The geese speak the same language.

Probably the snow geese think of the northern nesting ground as *theirs* and of the flyways and this lake as belonging to them, even though lately they have met strange obstacles during their autumnal flight. Jet planes hurtle past, and sometimes through *their* flights at *their* altitude. Tall buildings with bright lights rise into their flyway to confuse them. Ribbons of concrete slice through the virgin forests along their route. And here, at their resting place of centuries, men intent on mundane earthly pursuits such as growing barley have pumped their lakes and marshes nearly dry.

Nearly, but not quite. To the north there's a town. To the east there's a highway. To the south there's a mountain range. To the west there's a line of hunters. At this one place there's a sign. It says, "National Wildlife Refuge." The sign says this tiny spot still belongs to the geese.

So that's what so many geese are doing here all at once. There's no other place left for them to go.

SIOUX FALLS, SOUTH DAKOTA. Everywhere I've wandered across the Great Plains this summer, I have heard the clang of ringers and the clink of leaners coming from out behind the barn. Last week I watched a couple of farm boys playing horseshoes with *horseshoes,* discarded from the hooves of horses.

But, of course, there's a standardized item available down at the hardware store, and a little research has confirmed what I expected, that this rustic sport is now a big business. The St. Pierre Company of Worcester, Massachusetts—fancy name for a horseshoe firm—sells half a million dollars' worth of horseshoes every year that are meant for throwing, not for shoeing. The game may be played in the hay yard, but half a million ain't hay.

They say the Duke of Wellington and such an American aristocrat as George Washington indulged from time to time, but in the main this has always been a people's game, a barnyard substitute for tennis. I remember a gangling black kid who lived down the road in my rural youth, a farmer's son who hustled all the other farmers' sons for Orange Crushes, playing only as well as he had to play to win. He could throw ringers about half the time. The legendary horseshoe players of the Midwest could do far better than that. I am told that somewhere in Colorado lives an elderly man in a cowboy hat named Ted Allen, who came out of Natomas, Kansas, back in the thirties to demonstrate how the game should be played. Those who saw Ted Allen in his prime have never forgotten him. Once, they say, in a match with his arch rival, Fernando Isais of Gardena, California, Ted Allen ran off seventy-two straight ringers and broke Fernando's heart.

An annual World's Championship of Horseshoes is held. They're holding it next week, and they're hoping Ted Allen and Fernando Isais might drop by. That would be like a visit from Ruth and Gehrig or from Louis and Tunney, probably too much to hope for. I never met Ted Allen, and he is twenty years past his prime, and they say the smart money never bets against him.

It seems to me that every small town in this part of the country has a horseshoe player like that, a slow-talking old gent in overalls who will spot you two ringers and raise you two. Around here don't play for higher stakes than Orange Crushes.

MINNEAPOLIS, MINNESOTA. I hate to bring this up because I know you're trying to ignore it, but an antic quality has crept into American public life, a kind of lunacy that makes *Catch-22* look like the book of Elijah, a book of prophecy.

It may have started when the power companies said conserve power and we did, and they said their income had fallen as a result and raised their rates.

Then, there was that man in Chicago who went out to his garage and found a skunk in there. He found he couldn't keep the skunk; it's against the law to keep wild animals in Chicago. He couldn't give it away; that's against the law, too. He couldn't kill the skunk because, naturally, you can't kill wild animals in the city of Chicago. If you get a skunk in your garage in the city of Chicago, you can't do anything, except hope that the skunk goes away. I haven't heard whether the skunk has gone away yet.

The state of Minnesota, the other day, sent 100,000 pieces of mail, including a lot of state paychecks, over to the post office. The post office said, "Your account has insufficient funds; we're not going to mail this mail until you pay up." "But we sent you a check," the state of Minnesota said. "It's in the mail." You know, of course, what mail it was in. It was in the mail the post office wouldn't mail because it didn't have the check. Somebody from the state went over there and looked through 100,000 pieces of mail to find the only piece of mail that mattered.

This isn't the way things are supposed to work, but it's the way things are working. I saw a sign on the door of a café in Indiana. It said, "Open 24 hours a day, 7 days a week. Closed Thursday."